MznLnx

Missing Links Exam Preps

Exam Prep for

Management Strategy: Achieving Sustained Competitive Advantage

Marcus, 1st Edition

The MznLnx Exam Prep is your link from the texbook and lecture to your exams.
The MznLnx Exam Preps are unauthorized and comprehensive reviews of your textbooks.

All material provided by MznLnx and Rico Publications (c) 2010
Textbook publishers and textbook authors do not particpate in or contribute to these reviews.

MznLnx

Rico
Publications

Exam Prep for Management Strategy: Achieving Sustained Competitive Advantage
1st Edition
Marcus

Publisher: Raymond Houge
Assistant Editor: Michael Rouger
Text and Cover Designer: Lisa Buckner
Marketing Manager: Sara Swagger
Project Manager, Editorial Production: Jerry Emerson
Art Director: Vernon Lowerui

Product Manager: Dave Mason
Editorial Assitant: Rachel Guzmanji
Pedagogy: Debra Long
Cover Image: Jim Reed/Getty Images
Text and Cover Printer: City Printing, Inc.
Compositor: Media Mix, Inc.

(c) 2010 Rico Publications
ALL RIGHTS RESERVED. No part of this work
covered by the copyright may be reproduced or
used in any form or by an means--graphic, electronic,
or mechanical, including photocopying, recording,
taping, Web distribution, information storage, and
retrieval systems, or in any other manner--without the
written permission of the publisher.

Printed in the United States
ISBN:

For more information about our products, contact us at:
Dave.Mason@RicoPublications.com

For permission to use material from this text or
product, submit a request online to:
Dave.Mason@RicoPublications.com

Contents

CHAPTER 1
Strategy Basics — 1

CHAPTER 2
External Analysis — 11

CHAPTER 3
Internal Analysis — 25

CHAPTER 4
Timing and Positioning — 35

CHAPTER 5
Mergers, Acquisitions, and Divestitures — 42

CHAPTER 6
Globalization — 52

CHAPTER 7
Innovation and Entrepreneurship — 62

CHAPTER 8
Continuous Reinvention — 69

ANSWER KEY — 78

TO THE STUDENT

COMPREHENSIVE

The *MznLnx* Exam Prep series is designed to help you pass your exams. Editors at MznLnx review your textbooks and then prepare these practice exams to help you master the textbook material. Unlike study guides, workbooks, and practice tests provided by the texbook publisher and textbook authors, *MznLnx* gives you **all** of the material in each chapter in exam form, not just samples, so you can be sure to nail your exam.

MECHANICAL

The MznLnx Exam Prep series creates exams that will help you learn the subject matter as well as test you on your understanding. Each question is designed to help you master the concept. Just working through the exams, you gain an understanding of the subject--its a simple mechanical process that produces success.

INTEGRATED STUDY GUIDE AND REVIEW

MznLnx is not just a set of exams designed to test you, its also a comprehensive review of the subject content. Each exam question is also a review of the concept, making sure that you will get the answer correct without having to go to other sources of material. You learn as you go! Its the easiest way to pass an exam.

HUMOR

Studying can be tedious and dry. MznLnx's instructional design includes moderate humor within the exam questions on occassion, to break the tedium and revitalize the brain

Chapter 1. Strategy Basics

1. In economics, _____ refers to the ability of a person or a country to produce a particular good at a lower marginal cost and opportunity cost than another person or country. It is the ability to produce a product most efficiently given all the other products that could be produced. It can be contrasted with absolute advantage which refers to the ability of a person or a country to produce a particular good at a lower absolute cost than another.
    a. 28-hour day
    b. 1990 Clean Air Act
    c. 33 Strategies of War
    d. Comparative advantage

2. _____ is, in very basic words, a position a firm occupies against its competitors.

According to Michael Porter, the three methods for creating a sustainable _____ are through:

1. Cost leadership

2. Differentiation

3. Focus (economics)

    a. 28-hour day
    b. Competitive advantage
    c. Theory Z
    d. 1990 Clean Air Act

3. _____ refers to the aggregated strategies of single business firm or a strategic business unit (SBU) in a diversified corporation. According to Michael Porter, a firm must formulate a _____ that incorporates either cost leadership, differentiation or focus in order to achieve a sustainable competitive advantage and long-term success in its chosen arenas or industries.

Functional strategies include marketing strategies, new product development strategies, human resource strategies, financial strategies, legal strategies, supply-chain strategies, and information technology management strategies.

    a. Switching cost
    b. Competitive heterogeneity
    c. Strategic thinking
    d. Business strategy

4. In statistics, an _____ is an observation that is numerically distant from the rest of the data.

Chapter 1. Strategy Basics

They can occur by chance in any distribution, but they are often indicative either of measurement error or that the population has a heavy-tailed distribution. In the former case one wishes to discard them or use statistics that are robust to _____s, while in the latter case they indicate that the distribution has high kurtosis and that one should be very cautious in using tool or intuitions that assume a normal distribution.

  a. Outlier
  b. A Stake in the Outcome
  c. A4e
  d. AAAI

5. _____ is the process whereby an organization establishes the parameters within which programs, investments, and acquisitions are reaching the desired results. Performance Reference Model of the Federal Enterprise Architecture, 2005.

This process of measuring performance often requires the use of statistical evidence to determine progress toward specific defined organizational objectives.

There are many types of measurements.

  a. Performance measurement
  b. Workflow
  c. Crisis management
  d. CIFMS

6. The phrase mergers and _____s refers to the aspect of corporate strategy, corporate finance and management dealing with the buying, selling and combining of different companies that can aid, finance, or help a growing company in a given industry grow rapidly without having to create another business entity.

An _____, also known as a takeover or a buyout, is the buying of one company (the 'target') by another. An _____ may be friendly or hostile.

  a. A4e
  b. A Stake in the Outcome
  c. AAAI
  d. Acquisition

7. In finance and economics, _____ or divestiture is the reduction of some kind of asset for either financial or ethical objectives or sale of an existing business by a firm. A _____ is the opposite of an investment.

a. Divestment
b. 1990 Clean Air Act
c. 33 Strategies of War
d. 28-hour day

8. _____ in its literal sense is the process of transformation of local or regional phenomena into global ones. It can be described as a process by which the people of the world are unified into a single society and function together.

This process is a combination of economic, technological, sociocultural and political forces.

a. Histogram
b. Cost Management
c. Collaborative Planning, Forecasting and Replenishment
d. Globalization

9. In marketing, _____ has come to mean the process by which marketers try to create an image or identity in the minds of their target market for its product, brand, or organization. It is the 'relative competitive comparison' their product occupies in a given market as perceived by the target market.

Re-_____ involves changing the identity of a product, relative to the identity of competing products, in the collective minds of the target market.

a. Customer analytics
b. Context analysis
c. PEST analysis
d. Positioning

10. _____, known in the United States as antitrust law, has three main elements:

- prohibiting agreements or practices that restrict free trading and competition between business entities. This includes in particular the repression of cartels.
- banning abusive behavior by a firm dominating a market, or anti-competitive practices that tend to lead to such a dominant position. Practices controlled in this way may include predatory pricing, tying, price gouging, refusal to deal, and many others.
- supervising the mergers and acquisitions of large corporations, including some joint ventures. Transactions that are considered to threaten the competitive process can be prohibited altogether, or approved subject to 'remedies' such as an obligation to divest part of the merged business or to offer licenses or access to facilities to enable other businesses to continue competing.

The substance and practice of _____ varies from jurisdiction to jurisdiction. Protecting the interests of consumers (consumer welfare) and ensuring that entrepreneurs have an opportunity to compete in the market economy are often treated as important objectives. _____ is closely connected with law on deregulation of access to markets, state aids and subsidies, the privatization of state owned assets and the establishment of independent sector regulators. In recent decades, _____ has been viewed as a way to provide better public services.

   a. Right to Financial Privacy Act
   b. Competition law
   c. Rulemaking
   d. Federal Employers Liability Act

11. The loyalty business model is a business model used in strategic management in which company resources are employed so as to increase the loyalty of customers and other stakeholders in the expectation that corporate objectives will be met or surpassed. A typical example of this type of model is: quality of product or service leads to customer satisfaction, which leads to _____, which leads to profitability.

Fredrick Reichheld (1996) expanded the loyalty business model beyond customers and employees.

   a. 33 Strategies of War
   b. 1990 Clean Air Act
   c. Customer loyalty
   d. 28-hour day

12. _____, in microeconomics, are the cost advantages that a business obtains due to expansion. They are factors that cause a producer's average cost per unit to fall as scale is increased. _____ is a long run concept and refers to reductions in unit cost as the size of a facility, or scale, increases.
   a. A4e
   b. Economies of scale
   c. Economies of scope
   d. A Stake in the Outcome

13. _____ are conceptually similar to economies of scale. Whereas economies of scale primarily refer to efficiencies associated with supply-side changes, such as increasing or decreasing the scale of production, of a single product type, _____ refer to efficiencies primarily associated with demand-side changes, such as increasing or decreasing the scope of marketing and distribution, of different types of products. _____ are one of the main reasons for such marketing strategies as product bundling, product lining, and family branding.

Chapter 1. Strategy Basics

a. Economies of scope
b. Economies of scale
c. A4e
d. A Stake in the Outcome

14. _____, in strategic management and marketing is, according to Carlton O'Neal, the percentage or proportion of the total available market or market segment that is being serviced by a company. It can be expressed as a company's sales revenue (from that market) divided by the total sales revenue available in that market. It can also be expressed as a company's unit sales volume (in a market) divided by the total volume of units sold in that market.

a. Marketing plan
b. Green marketing
c. Business-to-business
d. Market share

15. _____ is a worldwide management consulting firm that focuses on solving issues of concern to senior management. McKinsey serves as an advisor to the world's leading businesses, governments, and institutions. It is widely recognized as a leader and one of the most prestigious firms in the management consulting industry.

a. 28-hour day
b. 33 Strategies of War
c. 1990 Clean Air Act
d. McKinsey ' Company

16. The _____ is an economic tool used to determine the strategic resources available to a firm. The fundamental principle of the _____ is that the basis for a competitive advantage of a firm lies primarily in the application of the bundle of valuable resources at the firm's disposal (Wernerfelt, 1984, p172; Rumelt, 1984, p557-558.) To transform a short-run competitive advantage into a sustained competitive advantage requires that these resources are heterogeneous in nature and not perfectly mobile (Barney, 1991, p105-106; Peteraf, 1993, p180).

a. Business philosophy
b. Frenemy
c. Catfish effect
d. Resource-based view

17. Network externalities resemble economies of scale, but they are not considered such because they are a function of the number of users of a good or service in an industry, not of the production efficiency within a business. _____ are only considered examples of network externalities if they are driven by demand side economies.

Formally, a production function $F(K,L)$ is defined to have:

- constant returns to scale if (for any constant a greater than or equal to 0) $F(aK, aL) = aF(K,L)$
- increasing returns to scale if (for any constant a greater than 1) $F(aK, aL) > aF(K,L)$
- decreasing returns to scale if (for any constant a greater than 1) $F(aK, aL) < aF(K,L)$

where K and L are factors of production, capital and labour, respectively.

As an example, the Cobb-Douglas functional form has constant returns to scale when the sum of the exponents adds up to one.

a. AAAI
b. A Stake in the Outcome
c. A4e
d. Economies of scale external to the firm

18. The phrase _____ refers to the aspect of corporate strategy, corporate finance and management dealing with the buying, selling and combining of different companies that can aid, finance, or help a growing company in a given industry grow rapidly without having to create another business entity.

An acquisition, also known as a takeover or a buyout, is the buying of one company (the 'target') by another. An acquisition may be friendly or hostile.

a. Mergers and acquisitions
b. 33 Strategies of War
c. 28-hour day
d. 1990 Clean Air Act

19. In business and accounting, _____s are everything of value that is owned by a person or company. Any property or object of value that one possesses, usually considered as applicable to the payment of one's debts is considered an _____. Simplistically stated, _____s are things of value that can be readily converted into cash.

a. AAAI
b. A Stake in the Outcome
c. A4e
d. Asset

20. _____ is the advantage gained by the initial occupant of a market segment. This advantage may stem from the fact that the first entrant can gain control of resources that followers may not be able to match. Sometimes the first mover is not able to capitalise on its advantage, leaving the opportunity for another firm to gain second-mover advantage.

   a. Horizontal integration
   b. Business ecosystem
   c. Customer retention
   d. First-mover advantage

21. The _____ is a performance management tool for measuring whether the smaller-scale operational activities of a company are aligned with its larger-scale objectives in terms of vision and strategy.

By focusing not only on financial outcomes but also on the operational, marketing and developmental inputs to these, the _____ helps provide a more comprehensive view of a business, which in turn helps organizations act in their best long-term interests. This tool is also being used to address business response to climate change and greenhouse gas emissions.

   a. Commercial management
   b. Balanced scorecard
   c. Middle management
   d. Management development

22. _____ refers to the movement of cash into or out of a business or financial product. It is usually measured during a specified, finite period of time. Measurement of _____ can be used

   - to determine a project's rate of return or value. The time of _____s into and out of projects are used as inputs in financial models such as internal rate of return, and net present value.
   - to determine problems with a business's liquidity. Being profitable does not necessarily mean being liquid. A company can fail because of a shortage of cash, even while profitable.
   - as an alternate measure of a business's profits when it is believed that accrual accounting concepts do not represent economic realities. For example, a company may be notionally profitable but generating little operational cash (as may be the case for a company that barters its products rather than selling for cash.) In such a case, the company may be deriving additional operating cash by issuing shares evaluating default risk, re-investment requirements, etc.

_____ is a generic term used differently depending on the context. It may be defined by users for their own purposes.

   a. Gross profit margin
   b. Gross profit
   c. Sweat equity
   d. Cash flow

23. _____, Gross profit margin or Gross Profit Rate can be defined as the amount of contribution to the business enterprise, after paying for direct-fixed and direct-variable unit costs, required to cover overheads (fixed commitments) and provide a buffer for unknown items. It expresses the relationship between gross profit and sales revenue.

It can be expressed in absolute terms:

Gross Profit = Revenue − Cost of Sales

or as the ratio of gross profit to sales revenue, usually in the form of a percentage:

_____ Percentage = (Revenue-Cost of Sales)/Revenue

Cost of Sales includes variable costs and fixed costs directly linked to the product, such as material and labor.

a. Gross margin
b. 1990 Clean Air Act
c. Profit maximization
d. Profit margin

24. An _____ is any party that makes an investment.

The term has taken on a specific meaning in finance to describe the particular types of people and companies that regularly purchase equity or debt securities for financial gain in exchange for funding an expanding company. Less frequently, the term is applied to parties who purchase real estate, currency, commodity derivatives, personal property, or other assets.

a. A4e
b. A Stake in the Outcome
c. AAAI
d. Investor

25. _____ or net present worth (NPW) is defined as the total present value (PV) of a time series of cash flows. It is a standard method for using the time value of money to appraise long-term projects. Used for capital budgeting, and widely throughout economics, it measures the excess or shortfall of cash flows, in present value terms, once financing charges are met.

a. 1990 Clean Air Act
b. Discounted cash flow
c. Present value
d. Net present value

26. The _____ percentage shows how profitable a company's assets are in generating revenue.

_____ can be computed as:

$$\text{ROA} = \frac{\text{Net Income + Interest Expense - Interest Tax savings}}{\text{Average Total Assets}}$$

This number tells you what the company can do with what it has, i.e. how many dollars of earnings they derive from each dollar of assets they control. Its a useful number for comparing competing companies in the same industry.

a. Return on equity
b. P/E ratio
c. Return on Capital Employed
d. Return on assets

27. The _____ of an edge is $c_f(u,v) = c(u,v) - f(u,v)$. This defines a residual network denoted $G_f(V, E_f)$, giving the amount of available capacity. See that there can be an edge from u to v in the residual network, even though there is no edge from u to v in the original network.

a. 1990 Clean Air Act
b. Residual capacity
c. 33 Strategies of War
d. 28-hour day

28. _____ is the value on a given date of a future payment or series of future payments, discounted to reflect the time value of money and other factors such as investment risk. _____ calculations are widely used in business and economics to provide a means to compare cash flows at different times on a meaningful 'like to like' basis.

If offered a choice between $100 today or $100 in one year, everyone will choose $100 today.

a. Present value
b. 1990 Clean Air Act
c. Net present value
d. Discounted cash flow

29. In corporate finance, _____ or _____ is an estimate of true economic profit after making corrective adjustments to GAAP accounting, including deducting the opportunity cost of equity capital. _____ can be measured as Net Operating Profit After Taxes(or NOPAT) less the money cost of capital. _____ is similar in nature to that of calculating another financial performance measure - Residual Income , however, there are a few complexities involved with coming up with the elements for calculating _____ over RI such as the myriad adjustments that might be made to NOPAT before it is suitable for the formula below.

a. A4e
b. Economic value added
c. AAAI
d. A Stake in the Outcome

30. _____ refers to the difference between the cost of materials purchased by a company plus the cost of the labor to assemble a product and the price at which the company sells the product. An example is the price of gasoline at the pump over the price of the oil in it. In national accounts used in macroeconomics, it refers to the contribution of the factors of production, i.e., land, labor, and capital goods, to raising the value of a product and corresponds to the incomes received by the owners of these factors.

a. Value added
b. Rehn-Meidner Model
c. Deregulation
d. Minimum wage

31. _____ are the earnings returned on the initial investment amount.

In the US, the Financial Accounting Standards Board (FASB) requires companies' income statements to report _____ for each of the major categories of the income statement: continuing operations, discontinued operations, extraordinary items, and net income.

The _____ formula does not include preferred dividends for categories outside of continued operations and net income.

a. A4e
b. AAAI
c. A Stake in the Outcome
d. Earnings per share

Chapter 2. External Analysis

1. _____ is, in very basic words, a position a firm occupies against its competitors.

According to Michael Porter, the three methods for creating a sustainable _____ are through:

1. Cost leadership

2. Differentiation

3. Focus (economics)

   a. Competitive Advantage
   b. 1990 Clean Air Act
   c. Theory Z
   d. 28-hour day

2. _____ is a worldwide management consulting firm that focuses on solving issues of concern to senior management. McKinsey serves as an advisor to the world's leading businesses, governments, and institutions. It is widely recognized as a leader and one of the most prestigious firms in the management consulting industry.
   a. 1990 Clean Air Act
   b. McKinsey ' Company
   c. 33 Strategies of War
   d. 28-hour day

3. In marketing, _____ has come to mean the process by which marketers try to create an image or identity in the minds of their target market for its product, brand, or organization. It is the 'relative competitive comparison' their product occupies in a given market as perceived by the target market.

Re-_____ involves changing the identity of a product, relative to the identity of competing products, in the collective minds of the target market.

   a. Context analysis
   b. PEST analysis
   c. Customer analytics
   d. Positioning

4. In economics and especially in the theory of competition, _____ are obstacles in the path of a firm that make it difficult to enter a given market.

_____ are the source of a firm's pricing power - the ability of a firm to raise prices without losing all its customers.

Chapter 2. External Analysis

The term refers to hindrances that an individual may face while trying to gain entrance into a profession or trade.

a. 28-hour day
b. Barriers to entry
c. Predatory pricing
d. 1990 Clean Air Act

5. In economics, a _____ exists when a specific individual or enterprise has sufficient control over a particular product or service to determine significantly the terms on which other individuals shall have access to it. Monopolies are thus characterized by a lack of economic competition for the good or service that they provide and a lack of viable substitute goods. The verb 'monopolize' refers to the process by which a firm gains persistently greater market share than what is expected under perfect competition.

a. 28-hour day
b. Monopoly
c. 1990 Clean Air Act
d. 33 Strategies of War

6. In neoclassical economics and microeconomics, _____ describes the perfect being a market in which there are many small firms, all producing homogeneous goods. In the short term, such markets are productively inefficient as output will not occur where marginal cost is equal to average cost, but allocatively efficient, as output under _____ will always occur where marginal cost is equal to marginal revenue, and therefore where marginal cost equals average revenue. However, in the long term, such markets are both allocatively and productively efficient.

a. Market structure
b. Deflation
c. Perfect competition
d. Gross domestic product

7. _____, net margin, net _____ or net profit ratio all refer to a measure of profitability. It is calculated by finding the net profit as a percentage of the revenue.

$$\text{Net profit margin} = \frac{\text{Net profit (after taxes)}}{\text{Revenue}} \times 100\%$$

The _____ is mostly used for internal comparison.

a. Profit maximization
b. Net profit margin
c. 1990 Clean Air Act
d. Profit margin

8. A _____ is a name or trademark connected with a product or producer. _____s have become increasingly important components of culture and the economy, now being described as 'cultural accessories and personal philosophies'.

Some people distinguish the psychological aspect of a _____ from the experiential aspect.

a. Brand awareness
b. Brand loyalty
c. Brand
d. Brand extension

9. A _____ is a set of exclusive rights granted by a state to an inventor or his assignee for a limited period of time in exchange for a disclosure of an invention.

The procedure for granting _____s, the requirements placed on the _____ee and the extent of the exclusive rights vary widely between countries according to national laws and international agreements. Typically, however, a _____ application must include one or more claims defining the invention which must be new, inventive, and useful or industrially applicable.

a. Patent
b. Food, Drug, and Cosmetic Act
c. Federal Trade Commission Act
d. Labor Management Reporting and Disclosure Act

10. _____ is one of the four Ps of the marketing mix. The other three aspects are product, promotion, and place. It is also a key variable in microeconomic price allocation theory.

a. Price floor
b. Penetration pricing
c. Transfer pricing
d. Pricing

Chapter 2. External Analysis

11. _____ is a term used in business to indicate a state of intense competitive rivalry accompanied by a multi-lateral series of price reduction. One competitor will lower its price, then others will lower their prices to match. If one of them reduces their price again, a new round of reductions starts.
    a. Pricing
    b. Price floor
    c. Price ceiling
    d. Price war

12. _____, in marketing, consists of a consumer's commitment to repurchase or otherwise continue using the brand and can be demonstrated by repeated buying of a product or service or other positive behaviors such as word of mouth advocacy.

    _____ is more than simple repurchasing, however. Customers may repurchase a brand due to situational constraints, a lack of viable alternatives, or out of convenience.

    a. Brand extension
    b. Brand image
    c. Brand loyalty
    d. Brand awareness

13. The _____ is a bank regulation, which sets a framework on how banks and depository institutions must handle their capital. The categorization of assets and capital is highly standardized so that it can be risk weighted. Internationally, the Basel Committee on Banking Supervision housed at the Bank for International Settlements influence each country's banking _____s.
    a. Lock box
    b. 1990 Clean Air Act
    c. Reserve requirement
    d. Capital requirement

14. _____, in microeconomics, are the cost advantages that a business obtains due to expansion. They are factors that cause a producer's average cost per unit to fall as scale is increased. _____ is a long run concept and refers to reductions in unit cost as the size of a facility, or scale, increases.
    a. A Stake in the Outcome
    b. A4e
    c. Economies of scope
    d. Economies of scale

15. In marketing, _____ is the process of distinguishing the differences of a product or offering from others, to make it more attractive to a particular target market. This involves differentiating it from competitors' products as well as one's own product offerings.

   a. Product differentiation
   b. Market development
   c. PEST analysis
   d. Market share

16. Network externalities resemble economies of scale, but they are not considered such because they are a function of the number of users of a good or service in an industry, not of the production efficiency within a business. _____ are only considered examples of network externalities if they are driven by demand side economies.

Formally, a production function F is defined to have:

- constant returns to scale if (for any constant a greater than or equal to 0) $F(aK, aL) = aF(K, L)$
- increasing returns to scale if (for any constant a greater than 1) $F(aK, aL) > aF(K, L)$
- decreasing returns to scale if (for any constant a greater than 1) $F(aK, aL) < aF(K, L)$

where K and L are factors of production, capital and labour, respectively.

As an example, the Cobb-Douglas functional form has constant returns to scale when the sum of the exponents adds up to one.

   a. AAAI
   b. Economies of scale external to the firm
   c. A Stake in the Outcome
   d. A4e

17. _____ is one of the four elements of marketing mix. An organization or set of organizations (go-betweens) involved in the process of making a product or service available for use or consumption by a consumer or business user.

The other three parts of the marketing mix are product, pricing, and promotion.

a. Missing completely at random
b. Matching theory
c. Job creation programs
d. Distribution

18. A variety of measures of national income and output are used in economics to estimate total economic activity in a country or region, including gross domestic product (GDP), _____ , and net national income (NNI.)

_____ is defined as the 'value of all (final) goods and services produced in a country in one year by the nationals, plus income earned by its citizens abroad,

a. 28-hour day
b. Gross national product
c. 1990 Clean Air Act
d. Purchasing power parity

19. _____ is the increase in the amount of the goods and services produced by an economy over time and is dependent on an increase in the creation of money. Growth is conventionally measured as the percent rate of increase in real gross domestic product, or real GDP. GDP is usually calculated in real terms, i.e. inflation-adjusted terms, in order to net out the effect of inflation on the price of the goods and services produced.
a. A Stake in the Outcome
b. Economic growth
c. AAAI
d. A4e

20. _____ is the process of social and economic change whereby a human group is transformed from a pre-industrial society into an industrial one. It is a part of a wider modernization process, where social change and economic development are closely related with technological innovation, particularly with the development of large-scale energy and metallurgy production. It is the extensive organization of an economy for the purpose of manufacturing.
a. Industrialization
b. A Stake in the Outcome
c. A4e
d. AAAI

21. _____ can be regarded as an outcome of mental processes (cognitive process) leading to the selection of a course of action among several alternatives. Every _____ process produces a final choice. The output can be an action or an opinion of choice.

a. Decision making
b. 28-hour day
c. 1990 Clean Air Act
d. 33 Strategies of War

22. _____ is a concept in ethics with several meanings. It is often used synonymously with such concepts as responsibility, answerability, enforcement, blameworthiness, liability and other terms associated with the expectation of account-giving. As an aspect of governance, it has been central to discussions related to problems in both the public and private (corporation) worlds.
a. Accountability
b. A Stake in the Outcome
c. Usury
d. A4e

23. _____, in strategic management and marketing is, according to Carlton O'Neal, the percentage or proportion of the total available market or market segment that is being serviced by a company. It can be expressed as a company's sales revenue (from that market) divided by the total sales revenue available in that market. It can also be expressed as a company's unit sales volume (in a market) divided by the total volume of units sold in that market.
a. Business-to-business
b. Marketing plan
c. Green marketing
d. Market share

24. _____ is a type of trade policy that allows traders to act and transact without interference from government. Thus, the policy permits trading partners mutual gains from trade, with goods and services produced according to the theory of comparative advantage.

Under a _____ policy, prices are a reflection of true supply and demand, and are the sole determinant of resource allocation.

a. 33 Strategies of War
b. 28-hour day
c. 1990 Clean Air Act
d. Free Trade

25. _____ is a designated group of countries that have agreed to eliminate tariffs, quotas and preferences on most (if not all) goods and services traded between them. It can be considered the second stage of economic integration. Countries choose this kind of economic integration form if their economical structures are complementary.

a. 1990 Clean Air Act
b. Free trade area
c. 33 Strategies of War
d. 28-hour day

26. The _____ or gross domestic income (GDI), a basic measure of an economy's economic performance, is the market value of all final goods and services made within the borders of a nation in a year. _____ can be defined in three ways, all of which are conceptually identical. First, it is equal to the total expenditures for all final goods and services produced within the country in a stipulated period of time (usually a 365-day year).
   a. Perfect competition
   b. Human capital
   c. Productivity management
   d. Gross domestic product

27. The _____ is a trilateral trade bloc in North America created by the governments of the United States, Canada, and Mexico. The agreement creating the trade bloc came into force on January 1, 1994. It superseded the Canada-United States Free Trade Agreement between the U.S. and Canada.
   a. Business war game
   b. Trade union
   c. Career portfolios
   d. North American Free Trade Agreement

28. The notion of _____ is found in the writings of Mikhail Bakunin, Friedrich Nietzsche, and in Werner Sombart's Krieg und Kapitalismus (War and Capitalism) (1913, p. 207), where he wrote: 'again out of destruction a new spirit of creativity arises'. In Capitalism, Socialism and Democracy, the Austrian economist Joseph Schumpeter popularized and used the term to describe the process of transformation that accompanies radical innovation.
   a. 1990 Clean Air Act
   b. Creative destruction
   c. 28-hour day
   d. 33 Strategies of War

29. An _____ is a statistic about the economy. _____s allow analysis of economic performance and predictions of future performance.

_____s include various indices, earnings reports, and economic summaries, such as unemployment, housing starts, Consumer Price Index (a measure for inflation), industrial production, bankruptcies, Gross Domestic Product, broadband internet penetration, retail sales, stock market prices, and money supply changes.

a. AAAI
b. A4e
c. A Stake in the Outcome
d. Economic indicator

30. _____ or _____ data refers to selected population characteristics as used in government, marketing or opinion research, or the _____ profiles used in such research. Note the distinction from the term 'demography' Commonly-used _____s include race, age, income, disabilities, mobility (in terms of travel time to work or number of vehicles available), educational attainment, home ownership, employment status, and even location.
a. Adam Smith
b. Affiliation
c. Demographic
d. Abraham Harold Maslow

31. In decision theory and estimation theory, the _____ of an estimator, $\hat{\theta}$, of an unknown parameter of the distribution, θ, is the expected value of the loss function

$$R(\theta, \hat{\theta}) = \mathbb{E}_\theta L(\theta, \hat{\theta}) = \int L(\theta, \hat{\theta}) \, dP_\theta.$$

where dP$_\theta$ is a probability measure parametrized by θ.

- For a scalar parameter θ and a quadratic loss function,

$$L(\theta, \hat{\theta}) = (\theta - \hat{\theta})^2$$

the _____ function becomes the mean squared error of the estimate,

$$R(\theta, \hat{\theta}) = E_\theta (\theta - \hat{\theta})^2$$

- In density estimation, the unknown parameter is probability density itself. The loss function is typically chosen to be a norm in an appropriate function space. For example, for L^2 norm,

$$L(f, \hat{f}) = \|f - \hat{f}\|_2^2$$

the _____ function becomes the mean integrated squared error

$$R(f, \hat{f}) = E\|f - \hat{f}\|^2$$

a. Risk aversion
b. Risk
c. Financial modeling
d. Linear model

32. _____ is the statistical study of all populations. It can be a very general science that can be applied to any kind of dynamic population, that is, one that changes over time or space It encompasses the study of the size, structure and distribution of populations, and spatial and/or temporal changes in them in response to birth, migration, aging and death.
   a. 1990 Clean Air Act
   b. 28-hour day
   c. 33 Strategies of War
   d. Demography

33. The term _____ was coined by the World Business Council for Sustainable Development (WBCSD) in its 1992 publication 'Changing Course'. It is based on the concept of creating more goods and services while using fewer resources and creating less waste and pollution.

The 1992 Earth Summit endorsed _____ as a means for companies to implement Agenda 21 in the private sector, and the term has become synonymous with a management philosophy geared towards sustainability.

a. A Stake in the Outcome
b. A4e
c. AAAI
d. Eco-efficiency

34. _____ is a pattern of resource use that aims to meet human needs while preserving the environment so that these needs can be met not only in the present, but also for future generations. The term was used by the Brundtland Commission which coined what has become the most often-quoted definition of _____ as development that 'meets the needs of the present without compromising the ability of future generations to meet their own needs.'

_____ ties together concern for the carrying capacity of natural systems with the social challenges facing humanity. As early as the 1970s 'sustainability' was employed to describe an economy 'in equilibrium with basic ecological support systems.' Ecologists have pointed to the 'limits of growth' and presented the alternative of a 'steady state economy' in order to address environmental concerns.

a. Global Reporting Initiative
b. Sustainability reporting
c. Sustainable business
d. Sustainable Development

35. _____ is exchange of capital, goods, and services across international borders or territories. In most countries, it represents a significant share of gross domestic product (GDP.) While _____ has been present throughout much of history, its economic, social, and political importance has been on the rise in recent centuries.

a. International trade
b. AAAI
c. A Stake in the Outcome
d. A4e

36. A _____ is an entity formed between two or more parties to undertake economic activity together. The parties agree to create a new entity by both contributing equity, and they then share in the revenues, expenses, and control of the enterprise. The venture can be for one specific project only, or a continuing business relationship such as the Fuji Xerox _____.

a. Joint venture
b. Meritor Savings Bank v. Vinson
c. Civil Rights Act of 1991
d. Patent

37. A _____ is a type of business entity in which partners (owners) share with each other the profits or losses of the business. _____s are often favored over corporations for taxation purposes, as the _____ structure does not generally incur a tax on profits before it is distributed to the partners (i.e. there is no dividend tax levied.) However, depending on the _____ structure and the jurisdiction in which it operates, owners of a _____ may be exposed to greater personal liability than they would as shareholders of a corporation.
   a. Mediation
   b. Partnership
   c. Due process
   d. Federal Employers Liability Act

38. _____ is a term used in project management and business administration to describe a process where all the individuals or groups that are likely to be affected by the activities of a project are identified and then sorted according to how much they can affect the project and how much the project can affect them. This information is used to assess how the interests of those stakeholders should be addressed in the project plan.

A stakeholder is any person or organization, who can be positively or negatively impacted by, or cause an impact on the actions of a company.

   a. Stakeholder analysis
   b. 28-hour day
   c. 33 Strategies of War
   d. 1990 Clean Air Act

39. An _____ is a person who has possession of an enterprise and assumes significant accountability for the inherent risks and the outcome. It is an ambitious leader who combines land, labor, and capital to create and market new goods or services. The term is a loanword from French and was first defined by the Irish economist Richard Cantillon.
   a. Entrepreneur
   b. AAAI
   c. A Stake in the Outcome
   d. A4e

40. A _____ is a relatively new executive level position at a corporation, company, organization typically reporting directly to the CEO or board of directors. The _____ is responsible for a brand's image, experience, and promise, and propagating it throughout all aspects of the company. The brand officer oversees marketing, advertising, design, public relations and customer service departments.
   a. Chief executive officer
   b. Director of communications
   c. Purchasing manager
   d. Chief brand officer

41. In political science and economics, the _____ or agency dilemma treats the difficulties that arise under conditions of incomplete and asymmetric information when a principal hires an agent, such as the problem that the two may not have the same interests, while the principal is, presumably, hiring the agent to pursue the interests of the former.

Various mechanisms may be used to try to align the interests of the agent with those of the principal, such as piece rates/commissions, profit sharing, efficiency wages, performance measurement (including financial statements), the agent posting a bond, or fear of firing. The _____ is found in most employer/employee relationships, for example, when stockholders hire top executives of corporations.

   a. Principal-agent problem
   b. 28-hour day
   c. 1990 Clean Air Act
   d. 33 Strategies of War

42. A _____ is a brief written statement of the purpose of a company or organization. Ideally, a _____ guides the actions of the organization, spells out its overall goal, provides a sense of direction, and guides decision making for all levels of management.

_____ s often contain the following:

- Purpose and aim of the organization
- The organization's primary stakeholders: clients, stockholders, etc.
- Responsibilities of the organization toward these stakeholders
- Products and services offered

In developing a _____:

- Encourage as much input as feasible from employees, volunteers, and other stakeholders
- Publicize it broadly

The _____ can be used to resolve differences between business stakeholders. Stakeholders include: employees including managers and executives, stockholders, board of directors, customers, suppliers, distributors, creditors, governments (local, state, federal, etc.), unions, competitors, NGO's, and the general public.

a. 1990 Clean Air Act
b. 28-hour day
c. 33 Strategies of War
d. Mission statement

43. In statistics, _____ is:

- the arithmetic _____
- the expected value of a random variable, which is also called the population _____.

It is sometimes stated that the '_____' _____s average. This is incorrect if '_____' is taken in the specific sense of 'arithmetic _____' as there are different types of averages: the _____, median, and mode. Other simple statistical analyses use measures of spread, such as range, interquartile range, or standard deviation. For a real-valued random variable X, the _____ is the expectation of X. Note that not every probability distribution has a defined _____; see the Cauchy distribution for an example.

a. Control chart
b. Statistical inference
c. Correlation
d. Mean

Chapter 3. Internal Analysis

1. _____ is something that a firm can do well and that meets the following three conditions:

Competencies are things that companys execute well across several business units or product sectors.

Firms usually have few competencies, but these are usually less liable to change rapidly.

   1. It provides consumer benefits
   2. It is not easy for competitors to imitate
   3. It can be leveraged widely to many products and markets.

A _____ can take various forms, including technical/subject matter know-how, a reliable process and/or close relationships with customers and suppliers (Mascarenhas et al. 1998.)

   a. Learning-by-doing
   b. NAIRU
   c. Dominant Design
   d. Core competency

2. A _____ is a body of elected or appointed members who jointly oversee the activities of a company or organization. The body sometimes has a different name, such as board of trustees, board of governors, board of managers, or executive board. It is often simply referred to as 'the board.'

A board's activities are determined by the powers, duties, and responsibilities delegated to it or conferred on it by an authority outside itself.

   a. Foreign Corrupt Practices Act
   b. Clean Water Act
   c. Competition law
   d. Board of directors

3. _____ has been described as the 'process of social influence in which one person can enlist the aid and support of others in the accomplishment of a common task' . A definition more inclusive of followers comes from Alan Keith of Genentech who said '_____ is ultimately about creating a way for people to contribute to making something extraordinary happen.'

_____ is one of the most salient aspects of the organizational context. However, defining _____ has been challenging.

Chapter 3. Internal Analysis

   a. Situational leadership
   b. Leadership
   c. 28-hour day
   d. 1990 Clean Air Act

4. The _____ is an economic tool used to determine the strategic resources available to a firm. The fundamental principle of the _____ is that the basis for a competitive advantage of a firm lies primarily in the application of the bundle of valuable resources at the firm's disposal (Wernerfelt, 1984, p172; Rumelt, 1984, p557-558.) To transform a short-run competitive advantage into a sustained competitive advantage requires that these resources are heterogeneous in nature and not perfectly mobile (Barney, 1991, p105-106; Peteraf, 1993, p180).
   a. Catfish effect
   b. Business philosophy
   c. Resource-based view
   d. Frenemy

5. _____ refers to bodies of techniques for investigating phenomena, acquiring new knowledge, or correcting and integrating previous knowledge. To be termed scientific, a method of inquiry must be based on gathering observable, empirical and measurable evidence subject to specific principles of reasoning. A _____ consists of the collection of data through observation and experimentation, and the formulation and testing of hypotheses.
   a. 33 Strategies of War
   b. 28-hour day
   c. 1990 Clean Air Act
   d. Scientific method

6. The _____ is a concept from business management that was first described and popularized by Michael Porter in his 1985 best-seller, Competitive Advantage: Creating and Sustaining Superior Performance.

A _____ is a chain of activities. Products pass through all activities of the chain in order and at each activity the product gains some value. The chain of activities gives the products more added value than the sum of added values of all activities. It is important not to mix the concept of the _____ with the costs occurring throughout the activities.

   a. Market development
   b. Value chain
   c. Mass marketing
   d. Customer relationship management

7. _____ is, in very basic words, a position a firm occupies against its competitors.

Chapter 3. Internal Analysis

According to Michael Porter, the three methods for creating a sustainable _____ are through:

1. Cost leadership

2. Differentiation

3. Focus (economics)

  a. Theory Z
  b. 1990 Clean Air Act
  c. 28-hour day
  d. Competitive advantage

8. _____ Movement refers to those researchers of organizational development who study the behavior of people in groups, in particular workplace groups. It originated in the 1920s' Hawthorne studies, which examined the effects of social relations, motivation and employee satisfaction on factory productivity. The movement viewed workers in terms of their psychology and fit with companies, rather than as interchangeable parts.
  a. Human relations
  b. Participatory management
  c. Work design
  d. Hersey-Blanchard situational theory

9. _____, widely known as F. W. Taylor, was an American mechanical engineer who sought to improve industrial efficiency. He is regarded as the father of scientific management, and was one of the first management consultants.

Taylor was one of the intellectual leaders of the Efficiency Movement and his ideas, broadly conceived, were highly influential in the Progressive Era.

  a. Frederick Winslow Taylor
  b. Douglas N. Daft
  c. Geoffrey Colvin
  d. Jonah Jacob Goldberg

10. _____ in Public Relations

There are different types of _____ in public relations; symmetric and asymmetric.

Two-way asymmetric public relations...>· can also be called 'scientific persuasion;'>· employs social science methods to develop more persuasive communication;>· generally focuses on achieving short-term attitude change;>· incorporates lots of feedback from target audiences and publics;>· is used by an organization primarily interested in having its publics come around to its way of thinking rather changing the organization, its policies, or its views.

Two-way symmetric public relations...>· relies on honest and open _____ and mutual give-and-take rather than one-way persuasion;>· focuses on mutual respect and efforts to achieve mutual understanding;>· emphasizes negotiation and a willingness to adapt and make compromises;>· requires organizations engaging in public relations to be willing to make significant adjustments in how they operate in order to accommodate their publics;>· seems to be used more by non-profit organizations, government agencies, and heavily regulated businesses such as public utilities than by competitive, profit-driven companies.

   a. Public relations
   b. 1990 Clean Air Act
   c. 28-hour day
   d. Two-way communication

11. The _____ is a standardized, on-scene, all-hazard incident management concept. It is a management protocol originally designed for emergency management agencies in the United States which was later federalized there. It has since been adopted by agencies in other countries.
   a. AAAI
   b. Incident Command Structure
   c. A Stake in the Outcome
   d. A4e

12. _____ is the state or fact of exclusive rights and control over property, which may be an object, land/real estate or intellectual property. An _____ right is also referred to as title. The concept of _____ has existed for thousands of years and in all cultures.
   a. A4e
   b. A Stake in the Outcome
   c. Emanation of the state
   d. Ownership

13. _____ is a class of behavioural theory that claims that there is no best way to organize a corporation, to lead a company, or to make decisions. Instead, the optimal course of action is contingent (dependant) upon the internal and external situation. Several contingency approaches were developed concurrently in the late 1960s.

a. Commercial management
b. Distributed management
c. Contingency theory
d. Capability management

14. _____ can be regarded as an outcome of mental processes (cognitive process) leading to the selection of a course of action among several alternatives. Every _____ process produces a final choice. The output can be an action or an opinion of choice.
a. Decision making
b. 1990 Clean Air Act
c. 33 Strategies of War
d. 28-hour day

15. _____ is an approach to leadership development, coined and defined by Robert Greenleaf and advanced by several authors such as Stephen Covey, Peter Block, Peter Senge, Max DePree, Margaret Wheatley, Ken Blanchard, and others. Servant-leadership emphasizes the leader's role as steward of the resources (human, financial and otherwise) provided by the organization. It encourages leaders to serve others while staying focused on achieving results in line with the organization's values and integrity.
a. Abraham Harold Maslow
b. Servant leadership
c. Affiliation
d. Adam Smith

16. Organizational culture is not the same as _____. It is wider and deeper concepts, something that an organization 'is' rather than what it 'has' (according to Buchanan and Huczynski.)

_____ is the total sum of the values, customs, traditions and meanings that make a company unique.

a. Path-goal theory
b. Work design
c. Job analysis
d. Corporate culture

17. _____ is a worldwide management consulting firm that focuses on solving issues of concern to senior management. McKinsey serves as an advisor to the world's leading businesses, governments, and institutions. It is widely recognized as a leader and one of the most prestigious firms in the management consulting industry.

a. 33 Strategies of War
b. 28-hour day
c. 1990 Clean Air Act
d. McKinsey ' Company

18. _____ according to Onuoha (2007) is the practice of starting new organizations or revitalizing mature organizations, particularly new businesses generally in response to identified opportunities. _____ is often a difficult undertaking, as a vast majority of new businesses fail. Entrepreneurial activities are substantially different depending on the type of organization that is being started.
   a. A Stake in the Outcome
   b. A4e
   c. AAAI
   d. Entrepreneurship

19. _____ is the management of the flow of goods, information and other resources, including energy and people, between the point of origin and the point of consumption in order to meet the requirements of consumers (frequently, and originally, military organizations.) _____ involves the integration of information, transportation, inventory, warehousing, material-handling, and packaging, and occasionally security. _____ is a channel of the supply chain which adds the value of time and place utility.
   a. Third-party logistics
   b. 28-hour day
   c. 1990 Clean Air Act
   d. Logistics

20. _____ is the strategic and coherent approach to the management of an organisation's most valued assets - the people working there who individually and collectively contribute to the achievement of the objectives of the business. The terms '_____' and 'human resources' (HR) have largely replaced the term 'personnel management' as a description of the processes involved in managing people in organizations. In simple sense, _____ means employing people, developing their resources, utilizing, maintaining and compensating their services in tune with the job and organizational requirement.
   a. Revolving door syndrome
   b. Progressive discipline
   c. Job knowledge
   d. Human resource management

21. _____ is an integrated communications-based process through which individuals and communities discover that existing and newly-identified needs and wants may be satisfied by the products and services of others.

_____ is defined by the American _____ Association as the activity, set of institutions, and processes for creating, communicating, delivering, and exchanging offerings that have value for customers, clients, partners, and society at large. The term developed from the original meaning which referred literally to going to market, as in shopping, or going to a market to buy or sell goods or services.

- a. Disruptive technology
- b. Marketing
- c. Market development
- d. Customer relationship management

22. _____ is an advertisement in which a particular product specifically mentions a competitor by name for the express purpose of showing why the competitor is inferior to the product naming it.

This should not be confused with parody advertisements, where a fictional product is being advertised for the purpose of poking fun at the particular advertisement, nor should it be confused with the use of a coined brand name for the purpose of comparing the product without actually naming an actual competitor. ('Wikipedia tastes better and is less filling than the Encyclopedia Galactica.')

In the 1980s, during what has been referred to as the cola wars, soft-drink manufacturer Pepsi ran a series of advertisements where people, caught on hidden camera, in a blind taste test, chose Pepsi over rival Coca-Cola.

- a. 33 Strategies of War
- b. 28-hour day
- c. 1990 Clean Air Act
- d. Comparative advertising

23. _____ is the acquisition of goods and/or services at the best possible total cost of ownership, in the right quality and quantity, at the right time, in the right place and from the right source for the direct benefit or use of corporations, individuals generally via a contract. Simple _____ may involve nothing more than repeat purchasing. Complex _____ could involve finding long term partners - or even 'co-destiny' suppliers that might fundamentally commit one organization to another.

- a. Sole proprietorship
- b. Psychological pricing
- c. Golden parachute
- d. Procurement

24. _____ is one of the four elements of marketing mix. An organization or set of organizations (go-betweens) involved in the process of making a product or service available for use or consumption by a consumer or business user.

The other three parts of the marketing mix are product, pricing, and promotion.

a. Job creation programs
b. Matching theory
c. Missing completely at random
d. Distribution

25. In economics, a _____ exists when a specific individual or enterprise has sufficient control over a particular product or service to determine significantly the terms on which other individuals shall have access to it. Monopolies are thus characterized by a lack of economic competition for the good or service that they provide and a lack of viable substitute goods. The verb 'monopolize' refers to the process by which a firm gains persistently greater market share than what is expected under perfect competition.
a. Monopoly
b. 33 Strategies of War
c. 1990 Clean Air Act
d. 28-hour day

26. In economics and especially in the theory of competition, _____ are obstacles in the path of a firm that make it difficult to enter a given market.

_____ are the source of a firm's pricing power - the ability of a firm to raise prices without losing all its customers.

The term refers to hindrances that an individual may face while trying to gain entrance into a profession or trade.

a. 28-hour day
b. Predatory pricing
c. Barriers to entry
d. 1990 Clean Air Act

27. There are many important decisions about product and service development and marketing. In the process of product development and marketing we should focus on strategic decisions about product attributes, product branding, product packaging, product labeling and product support services. But product strategy also calls for building a _____.
a. Product bundling
b. Marketing strategy
c. Product line
d. Context analysis

Chapter 3. Internal Analysis

28. _____ refers to the process of screening, and selecting qualified people for a job at an organization or firm mid- and large-size organizations and companies often retain professional recruiters or outsource some of the process to _____ agencies. External _____ is the process of attracting and selecting employees from outside the organization.

The _____ industry has four main types of agencies: employment agencies, _____ websites and job search engines, 'headhunters' for executive and professional _____, and in-house _____.

   a. Labour hire
   b. Recruitment
   c. Referral recruitment
   d. Recruitment Process Outsourcing

29. _____ refers to increasing the spiritual, political, social or economic strength of individuals and communities. It often involves the empowered developing confidence in their own capacities.

The term Human _____ covers a vast landscape of meanings, interpretations, definitions and disciplines ranging from psychology and philosophy to the highly commercialized Self-Help industry and Motivational sciences.

   a. A4e
   b. A Stake in the Outcome
   c. AAAI
   d. Empowerment

30. The loyalty business model is a business model used in strategic management in which company resources are employed so as to increase the loyalty of customers and other stakeholders in the expectation that corporate objectives will be met or surpassed. A typical example of this type of model is: quality of product or service leads to customer satisfaction, which leads to _____, which leads to profitability.

Fredrick Reichheld (1996) expanded the loyalty business model beyond customers and employees.

   a. 1990 Clean Air Act
   b. 28-hour day
   c. 33 Strategies of War
   d. Customer loyalty

31. A _____ is a process in which a potential employee is evaluated by an employer for prospective employment in their company, organization and was established in the late 16th century.

A _____ typically precedes the hiring decision, and is used to evaluate the candidate. The interview is usually preceded by the evaluation of submitted résumés from interested candidates, then selecting a small number of candidates for interviews.

a. Payrolling
b. Supported employment
c. Split shift
d. Job interview

32. The phrase mergers and _____s refers to the aspect of corporate strategy, corporate finance and management dealing with the buying, selling and combining of different companies that can aid, finance, or help a growing company in a given industry grow rapidly without having to create another business entity.

An _____, also known as a takeover or a buyout, is the buying of one company (the 'target') by another. An _____ may be friendly or hostile.

a. A Stake in the Outcome
b. A4e
c. AAAI
d. Acquisition

33. In marketing, _____ has come to mean the process by which marketers try to create an image or identity in the minds of their target market for its product, brand, or organization. It is the 'relative competitive comparison' their product occupies in a given market as perceived by the target market.

Re-_____ involves changing the identity of a product, relative to the identity of competing products, in the collective minds of the target market.

a. PEST analysis
b. Context analysis
c. Positioning
d. Customer analytics

Chapter 4. Timing and Positioning

1. _____ is the advantage gained by the initial occupant of a market segment. This advantage may stem from the fact that the first entrant can gain control of resources that followers may not be able to match. Sometimes the first mover is not able to capitalise on its advantage, leaving the opportunity for another firm to gain second-mover advantage.

   a. Business ecosystem
   b. Customer retention
   c. Horizontal integration
   d. First-mover advantage

2. _____ is the study of how the variation (uncertainty) in the output of a mathematical model can be apportioned, qualitatively or quantitatively, to different sources of variation in the input of a model.

   In more general terms uncertainty and sensitivity analyses investigate the robustness of a study when the study includes some form of mathematical modelling. While uncertainty analysis studies the overall uncertainty in the conclusions of the study, _____ tries to identify what source of uncertainty weights more on the study's conclusions.

   a. Foreign ownership
   b. Policies and procedures
   c. No-bid contract
   d. Sensitivity analysis

3. In marketing, _____ has come to mean the process by which marketers try to create an image or identity in the minds of their target market for its product, brand, or organization. It is the 'relative competitive comparison' their product occupies in a given market as perceived by the target market.

   Re-_____ involves changing the identity of a product, relative to the identity of competing products, in the collective minds of the target market.

   a. Customer analytics
   b. PEST analysis
   c. Context analysis
   d. Positioning

4. _____ is, in very basic words, a position a firm occupies against its competitors.

   According to Michael Porter, the three methods for creating a sustainable _____ are through:

   1. Cost leadership

   2. Differentiation

3. Focus (economics)

   a. 1990 Clean Air Act
   b. Competitive advantage
   c. Theory Z
   d. 28-hour day

5. In economics, business, retail, and accounting, a _____ is the value of money that has been used up to produce something, and hence is not available for use anymore. In economics, a _____ is an alternative that is given up as a result of a decision. In business, the _____ may be one of acquisition, in which case the amount of money expended to acquire it is counted as _____.

   a. Cost
   b. Cost allocation
   c. Fixed costs
   d. Cost overrun

6. _____ is a concept developed by Michael Porter, used in business strategy. It describes a way to establish the competitive advantage. _____, in basic words, means the lowest cost of operation in the industry.

   a. Strategic group
   b. Switching cost
   c. Strategic business unit
   d. Cost leadership

7. _____ has been described as the 'process of social influence in which one person can enlist the aid and support of others in the accomplishment of a common task'. A definition more inclusive of followers comes from Alan Keith of Genentech who said '_____ is ultimately about creating a way for people to contribute to making something extraordinary happen.'

   _____ is one of the most salient aspects of the organizational context. However, defining _____ has been challenging.

   a. Leadership
   b. Situational leadership
   c. 28-hour day
   d. 1990 Clean Air Act

Chapter 4. Timing and Positioning

8. _____ is an advertisement in which a particular product specifically mentions a competitor by name for the express purpose of showing why the competitor is inferior to the product naming it.

This should not be confused with parody advertisements, where a fictional product is being advertised for the purpose of poking fun at the particular advertisement, nor should it be confused with the use of a coined brand name for the purpose of comparing the product without actually naming an actual competitor. ('Wikipedia tastes better and is less filling than the Encyclopedia Galactica.')

In the 1980s, during what has been referred to as the cola wars, soft-drink manufacturer Pepsi ran a series of advertisements where people, caught on hidden camera, in a blind taste test, chose Pepsi over rival Coca-Cola.

   a. 33 Strategies of War
   b. 28-hour day
   c. 1990 Clean Air Act
   d. Comparative advertising

9. _____ is a theory of management that analyzes and synthesizes workflows, with the objective of improving labour productivity. The core ideas of the theory were developed by Frederick Winslow Taylor in the 1880s and 1890s, and were first published in his monographs, Shop Management and The Principles of _____ Taylor believed that decisions based upon tradition and rules of thumb should be replaced by precise procedures developed after careful study of an individual at work.

   a. Capacity planning
   b. Master production schedule
   c. Scientific management
   d. Value engineering

10. _____, widely known as F. W. Taylor, was an American mechanical engineer who sought to improve industrial efficiency. He is regarded as the father of scientific management, and was one of the first management consultants.

Taylor was one of the intellectual leaders of the Efficiency Movement and his ideas, broadly conceived, were highly influential in the Progressive Era.

   a. Douglas N. Daft
   b. Jonah Jacob Goldberg
   c. Frederick Winslow Taylor
   d. Geoffrey Colvin

Chapter 4. Timing and Positioning

11. _____ or lean production, which is often known simply as 'Lean', is a production practice that considers the expenditure of resources for any goal other than the creation of value for the end customer to be wasteful, and thus a target for elimination. Working from the perspective of the customer who consumes a product or service, 'value' is defined as any action or process that a customer would be willing to pay for. Basically, lean is centered around creating more value with less work.
    a. Theory of constraints
    b. Production line
    c. Six Sigma
    d. Lean manufacturing

12. _____, in strategic management and marketing is, according to Carlton O'Neal, the percentage or proportion of the total available market or market segment that is being serviced by a company. It can be expressed as a company's sales revenue (from that market) divided by the total sales revenue available in that market. It can also be expressed as a company's unit sales volume (in a market) divided by the total volume of units sold in that market.
    a. Marketing plan
    b. Business-to-business
    c. Market share
    d. Green marketing

13. In marketing, _____ is the process of distinguishing the differences of a product or offering from others, to make it more attractive to a particular target market. This involves differentiating it from competitors' products as well as one's own product offerings.
    a. PEST analysis
    b. Market development
    c. Market share
    d. Product differentiation

14. _____ is a business management strategy aimed at embedding awareness of quality in all organizational processes. _____ has been widely used in manufacturing, education, hospitals, call centers, government, and service industries, as well as NASA space and science programs.

As defined by the International Organization for Standardization (ISO):

> '_____ is a management approach for an organization, centered on quality, based on the participation of all its members and aiming at long-term success through customer satisfaction, and benefits to all members of the organization and to society.' ISO 8402:1994

One major aim is to reduce variation from every process so that greater consistency of effort is obtained. (Royse, D., Thyer, B., Padgett D., ' Logan T., 2006)

Chapter 4. Timing and Positioning

a. Quality management
b. 1990 Clean Air Act
c. 28-hour day
d. Total quality management

15. _____ can be considered to have three main components: quality control, quality assurance and quality improvement. _____ is focused not only on product quality, but also the means to achieve it. _____ therefore uses quality assurance and control of processes as well as products to achieve more consistent quality.

a. 1990 Clean Air Act
b. Quality management
c. 28-hour day
d. Total quality management

16. _____ is an inventory strategy that strives to improve the return on investment of a business by reducing in-process inventory and its associated carrying costs. To meet _____ objectives, the process relies on signals between different points in the process. This means the process is often driven by a series of signals, or Kanban, which tell production when to make the next part. Kanban are usually 'tickets' but can be simple visual signals, such as the presence or absence of a part on a shelf. Implemented correctly, _____ can dramatically improve a manufacturing organization's return on investment, quality, and efficiency.

a. 28-hour day
b. 1990 Clean Air Act
c. 33 Strategies of War
d. Just-in-time

17. In business and engineering, new _____ is the term used to describe the complete process of bringing a new product or service to market. There are two parallel paths involved in the NProduct development process: one involves the idea generation, product design, and detail engineering; the other involves market research and marketing analysis. Companies typically see new _____ as the first stage in generating and commercializing new products within the overall strategic process of product life cycle management used to maintain or grow their market share.

a. 33 Strategies of War
b. 1990 Clean Air Act
c. 28-hour day
d. Product development

18. _____ refers to the movement of cash into or out of a business or financial product. It is usually measured during a specified, finite period of time. Measurement of _____ can be used

- to determine a project's rate of return or value. The time of _____s into and out of projects are used as inputs in financial models such as internal rate of return, and net present value.
- to determine problems with a business's liquidity. Being profitable does not necessarily mean being liquid. A company can fail because of a shortage of cash, even while profitable.
- as an alternate measure of a business's profits when it is believed that accrual accounting concepts do not represent economic realities. For example, a company may be notionally profitable but generating little operational cash (as may be the case for a company that barters its products rather than selling for cash.) In such a case, the company may be deriving additional operating cash by issuing shares evaluating default risk, re-investment requirements, etc.

_____ is a generic term used differently depending on the context. It may be defined by users for their own purposes.

a. Cash flow
b. Sweat equity
c. Gross profit
d. Gross profit margin

19. A _____ is the system of organizations, people, technology, activities, information and resources involved in moving a product or service from supplier to customer. _____ activities transform natural resources, raw materials and components into a finished product that is delivered to the end customer. In sophisticated _____ systems, used products may re-enter the _____ at any point where residual value is recyclable.

a. Wholesalers
b. Drop shipping
c. Packaging
d. Supply chain

20. Procter is a surname, and may also refer to:

- Bryan Waller Procter (pseud. Barry Cornwall), English poet
- Goodwin Procter, American law firm
- _____, consumer products multinational

a. Strict liability
b. Master and Servant Acts
c. Downstream
d. Procter ' Gamble

21. A _____ is a concept used in strategic management that groups companies within an industry that have similar business models or similar combinations of strategies. For example, the restaurant industry can be divided into several _____s including fast-food and fine-dining based on variables such as preparation time, pricing, and presentation. The number of groups within an industry and their composition depends on the dimensions used to define the groups.
   a. Corporate strategy
   b. Strategic group
   c. Strategic drift
   d. Strategic business unit

22. In economics and especially in the theory of competition, _____ are obstacles in the path of a firm that make it difficult to enter a given market.

_____ are the source of a firm's pricing power - the ability of a firm to raise prices without losing all its customers.

The term refers to hindrances that an individual may face while trying to gain entrance into a profession or trade.

   a. 28-hour day
   b. 1990 Clean Air Act
   c. Predatory pricing
   d. Barriers to entry

23. _____ is one of the four elements of marketing mix. An organization or set of organizations (go-betweens) involved in the process of making a product or service available for use or consumption by a consumer or business user.

The other three parts of the marketing mix are product, pricing, and promotion.

   a. Matching theory
   b. Missing completely at random
   c. Distribution
   d. Job creation programs

Chapter 5. Mergers, Acquisitions, and Divestitures

1. The phrase mergers and _____s refers to the aspect of corporate strategy, corporate finance and management dealing with the buying, selling and combining of different companies that can aid, finance, or help a growing company in a given industry grow rapidly without having to create another business entity.

An _____, also known as a takeover or a buyout, is the buying of one company (the 'target') by another. An _____ may be friendly or hostile.

   a. AAAI
   b. A4e
   c. A Stake in the Outcome
   d. Acquisition

2. _____ refers to the aggregated strategies of single business firm or a strategic business unit (SBU) in a diversified corporation. According to Michael Porter, a firm must formulate a _____ that incorporates either cost leadership, differentiation or focus in order to achieve a sustainable competitive advantage and long-term success in its chosen arenas or industries.

Functional strategies include marketing strategies, new product development strategies, human resource strategies, financial strategies, legal strategies, supply-chain strategies, and information technology management strategies.

   a. Strategic thinking
   b. Business strategy
   c. Switching cost
   d. Competitive heterogeneity

3. In finance and economics, _____ or divestiture is the reduction of some kind of asset for either financial or ethical objectives or sale of an existing business by a firm. A _____ is the opposite of an investment.
   a. 33 Strategies of War
   b. Divestment
   c. 28-hour day
   d. 1990 Clean Air Act

4. In microeconomics and strategic management, the term _____ describes a type of ownership and control. It is a strategy used by a business or corporation that seeks to sell a type of product in numerous markets. _____ in marketing is much more common than vertical integration is in production.

Chapter 5. Mergers, Acquisitions, and Divestitures

a. Career development
b. Farmshoring
c. No-bid contract
d. Horizontal integration

5. A _____ is an entity formed between two or more parties to undertake economic activity together. The parties agree to create a new entity by both contributing equity, and they then share in the revenues, expenses, and control of the enterprise. The venture can be for one specific project only, or a continuing business relationship such as the Fuji Xerox _____.

a. Civil Rights Act of 1991
b. Meritor Savings Bank v. Vinson
c. Joint venture
d. Patent

6. In law, _____ refers to the process by which a company (or part of a company) is brought to an end, and the assets and property of the company redistributed. _____ can also be referred to as winding-up or dissolution, although dissolution technically refers to the last stage of _____. The process of _____ also arises when customs, an authority or agency in a country responsible for collecting and safeguarding customs duties, determines the final computation or ascertainment of the duties or drawback accruing on an entry.

a. 33 Strategies of War
b. 28-hour day
c. 1990 Clean Air Act
d. Liquidation

7. The _____ is a concept from business management that was first described and popularized by Michael Porter in his 1985 best-seller, Competitive Advantage: Creating and Sustaining Superior Performance.

A _____ is a chain of activities. Products pass through all activities of the chain in order and at each activity the product gains some value. The chain of activities gives the products more added value than the sum of added values of all activities. It is important not to mix the concept of the _____ with the costs occurring throughout the activities.

a. Customer relationship management
b. Market development
c. Mass marketing
d. Value chain

Chapter 5. Mergers, Acquisitions, and Divestitures

8. In microeconomics and management, the term _____ describes a style of management control. Vertically integrated companies are united through a hierarchy with a common owner. Usually each member of the hierarchy produces a different product or (market-specific) service, and the products combine to satisfy a common need.
   a. 1990 Clean Air Act
   b. 33 Strategies of War
   c. 28-hour day
   d. Vertical integration

9. A _____ is a process in which a potential employee is evaluated by an employer for prospective employment in their company, organization and was established in the late 16th century.

A _____ typically precedes the hiring decision, and is used to evaluate the candidate. The interview is usually preceded by the evaluation of submitted résumés from interested candidates, then selecting a small number of candidates for interviews.

   a. Split shift
   b. Payrolling
   c. Supported employment
   d. Job interview

10. An _____ is a person who has possession of an enterprise and assumes significant accountability for the inherent risks and the outcome. It is an ambitious leader who combines land, labor, and capital to create and market new goods or services. The term is a loanword from French and was first defined by the Irish economist Richard Cantillon.
    a. Entrepreneur
    b. AAAI
    c. A4e
    d. A Stake in the Outcome

11. _____ is a worldwide management consulting firm that focuses on solving issues of concern to senior management. McKinsey serves as an advisor to the world's leading businesses, governments, and institutions. It is widely recognized as a leader and one of the most prestigious firms in the management consulting industry.
    a. 1990 Clean Air Act
    b. 28-hour day
    c. 33 Strategies of War
    d. McKinsey ' Company

Chapter 5. Mergers, Acquisitions, and Divestitures

12. _____ is the removal or simplification of government rules and regulations that constrain the operation of market forces. _____ does not mean elimination of laws against fraud, but eliminating or reducing government control of how business is done, thereby moving toward a more free market.

The stated rationale for '_____' is often that fewer and simpler regulations will lead to a raised level of competitiveness, therefore higher productivity, more efficiency and lower prices overall.

   a. Value added
   b. Natural rate of unemployment
   c. Rehn-Meidner Model
   d. Deregulation

13. _____ in its literal sense is the process of transformation of local or regional phenomena into global ones. It can be described as a process by which the people of the world are unified into a single society and function together.

This process is a combination of economic, technological, sociocultural and political forces.

   a. Cost Management
   b. Histogram
   c. Collaborative Planning, Forecasting and Replenishment
   d. Globalization

14. _____ is the incidence or process of transferring ownership of a business, enterprise, agency or public service from the public sector (government) to the private sector (business.) In a broader sense, _____ refers to transfer of any government function to the private sector including governmental functions like revenue collection and law enforcement.

   a. Performance reports
   b. Privatization
   c. 28-hour day
   d. 1990 Clean Air Act

15. The phrase _____ refers to the aspect of corporate strategy, corporate finance and management dealing with the buying, selling and combining of different companies that can aid, finance, or help a growing company in a given industry grow rapidly without having to create another business entity.

An acquisition, also known as a takeover or a buyout, is the buying of one company (the 'target') by another. An acquisition may be friendly or hostile.

a. 28-hour day
b. Mergers and acquisitions
c. 1990 Clean Air Act
d. 33 Strategies of War

16. _____, known in the United States as antitrust law, has three main elements:

- prohibiting agreements or practices that restrict free trading and competition between business entities. This includes in particular the repression of cartels.
- banning abusive behavior by a firm dominating a market, or anti-competitive practices that tend to lead to such a dominant position. Practices controlled in this way may include predatory pricing, tying, price gouging, refusal to deal, and many others.
- supervising the mergers and acquisitions of large corporations, including some joint ventures. Transactions that are considered to threaten the competitive process can be prohibited altogether, or approved subject to 'remedies' such as an obligation to divest part of the merged business or to offer licenses or access to facilities to enable other businesses to continue competing.

The substance and practice of _____ varies from jurisdiction to jurisdiction. Protecting the interests of consumers (consumer welfare) and ensuring that entrepreneurs have an opportunity to compete in the market economy are often treated as important objectives. _____ is closely connected with law on deregulation of access to markets, state aids and subsidies, the privatization of state owned assets and the establishment of independent sector regulators. In recent decades, _____ has been viewed as a way to provide better public services.

a. Federal Employers Liability Act
b. Right to Financial Privacy Act
c. Rulemaking
d. Competition law

17. _____ are the earnings returned on the initial investment amount.

In the US, the Financial Accounting Standards Board (FASB) requires companies' income statements to report _____ for each of the major categories of the income statement: continuing operations, discontinued operations, extraordinary items, and net income.

The _____ formula does not include preferred dividends for categories outside of continued operations and net income.

Chapter 5. Mergers, Acquisitions, and Divestitures

a. A Stake in the Outcome
b. Earnings per share
c. AAAI
d. A4e

18. The _____ is a United States federal law signed into law on October 24, 1978. The main purpose of the act was to remove government control over fares, routes and market entry (of new airlines) from commercial aviation.

a. A Stake in the Outcome
b. A4e
c. AAAI
d. Airline Deregulation Act

19. The _____ was a regulatory body in the United States created by the Interstate Commerce Act of 1887, which was signed into law by President Grover Cleveland. The agency was abolished in 1995, and the agency's remaining functions were transferred to the Surface Transportation Board.

The Commission's five members were appointed by the President with the consent of the United States Senate.

a. Interstate Commerce Commission
b. Extended Enterprise
c. American Institute of Industrial Engineers
d. United States Department of Agriculture

20. _____ is something that a firm can do well and that meets the following three conditions:

Competencies are things that companys execute well across several business units or product sectors.

Firms usually have few competencies, but these are usually less liable to change rapidly.

1. It provides consumer benefits
2. It is not easy for competitors to imitate
3. It can be leveraged widely to many products and markets.

A _____ can take various forms, including technical/subject matter know-how, a reliable process and/or close relationships with customers and suppliers (Mascarenhas et al. 1998.)

Chapter 5. Mergers, Acquisitions, and Divestitures

a. NAIRU
b. Core competency
c. Learning-by-doing
d. Dominant Design

21. _____ is an integrated communications-based process through which individuals and communities discover that existing and newly-identified needs and wants may be satisfied by the products and services of others.

_____ is defined by the American _____ Association as the activity, set of institutions, and processes for creating, communicating, delivering, and exchanging offerings that have value for customers, clients, partners, and society at large. The term developed from the original meaning which referred literally to going to market, as in shopping, or going to a market to buy or sell goods or services.

a. Market development
b. Disruptive technology
c. Customer relationship management
d. Marketing

22. _____ are conceptually similar to economies of scale. Whereas economies of scale primarily refer to efficiencies associated with supply-side changes, such as increasing or decreasing the scale of production, of a single product type, _____ refer to efficiencies primarily associated with demand-side changes, such as increasing or decreasing the scope of marketing and distribution, of different types of products. _____ are one of the main reasons for such marketing strategies as product bundling, product lining, and family branding.

a. Economies of scale
b. Economies of scope
c. A Stake in the Outcome
d. A4e

23. _____ is the term used to describe a situation where different entities cooperate advantageously for a final outcome. Simply defined, it means that the whole is greater than the sum of the individual parts. Although the whole will be greater than each individual part, this is not the concept of _____.

a. Synergy
b. 28-hour day
c. 33 Strategies of War
d. 1990 Clean Air Act

Chapter 5. Mergers, Acquisitions, and Divestitures

24. The _____ is a chart that had been created by Bruce Henderson for the Boston Consulting Group in 1970 to help corporations with analyzing their business units or product lines. This helps the company allocate resources and is used as an analytical tool in brand marketing, product management, strategic management, and portfolio analysis. _____

To use the chart, analysts plot a scatter graph to rank the business units (or products) on the basis of their relative market shares and growth rates.

   a. Marketing strategy
   b. BCG Matrix
   c. Marketing plan
   d. Market segment

25. In business, a _____ is a product or a business unit that generates unusually high profit margins: so high that it is responsible for a large amount of a company's operating profit. This profit far exceeds the amount necessary to maintain the _____ business, and the excess is used by the business for other purposes.

A firm is said to be acting as a _____ when its earnings per share (EPS) is equal to its dividends per share (DPS), or in other words, when a firm pays out 100% of its free cash flow (FCF) to its shareholders as dividends at the end of each accounting term.

   a. Workflow
   b. Middle management
   c. Design management in organization
   d. Cash cow

26. _____ is a strategic planning method used to evaluate the Strengths, Weaknesses, Opportunities, and Threats involved in a project or in a business venture. It involves specifying the objective of the business venture or project and identifying the internal and external factors that are favorable and unfavorable to achieving that objective. The technique is credited to Albert Humphrey, who led a convention at Stanford University in the 1960s and 1970s using data from Fortune 500 companies.
   a. Corporate image
   b. Market share
   c. Marketing
   d. SWOT analysis

Chapter 5. Mergers, Acquisitions, and Divestitures

27. The _____ (Situation, Task, Action, Result) format is a job interview technique used by interviewers to gather all the relevant information about a specific capability that the job requires. This interview format is said to have a higher degree of predictability of future on-the-job performance than the traditional interview.

- Situation: The interviewer wants you to present a recent challenge and situation in which you found yourself.
- Task: What did you have to achieve? The interviewer will be looking to see what you were trying to achieve from the situation.
- Action: What did you do? The interviewer will be looking for information on what you did, why you did it and what were the alternatives.
- Results: What was the outcome of your actions? What did you achieve through your actions and did you meet your objectives. What did you learn from this experience and have you used this learning since?

a. Star
b. Rasch models
c. Phrase completion
d. Competency-based job descriptions

28. _____, in strategic management and marketing is, according to Carlton O'Neal, the percentage or proportion of the total available market or market segment that is being serviced by a company. It can be expressed as a company's sales revenue (from that market) divided by the total sales revenue available in that market. It can also be expressed as a company's unit sales volume (in a market) divided by the total volume of units sold in that market.

a. Business-to-business
b. Market share
c. Marketing plan
d. Green marketing

29. _____ is a term in management and corporate restructuring that refers to a planned reduction in the number of layers of a management hierarchy.

a. Supervisory board
b. Product innovation
c. Mass market
d. Delayering

30. _____ refers to the methods of practicing and using another person's business philosophy. The franchisor grants the independent operator the right to distribute its products, techniques, and trademarks for a percentage of gross monthly sales and a royalty fee. Various tangibles and intangibles such as national or international advertising, training, and other support services are commonly made available by the franchisor.

Chapter 5. Mergers, Acquisitions, and Divestitures

a. ServiceMaster
b. Franchising
c. 1990 Clean Air Act
d. 28-hour day

31. _____ are assets, infrastructure or capabilities needed to support the successful commercialization and marketing of a technological innovation, other than those assets fundamentally associated with that innovation. The term was first coined by David Teece. Key empirical studies on _____ were conducted by Frank T. Rothaermel.
    a. Hypercompetition
    b. NAIRU
    c. Complementary assets
    d. Core competency

32. In business and accounting, _____s are everything of value that is owned by a person or company. Any property or object of value that one possesses, usually considered as applicable to the payment of one's debts is considered an _____. Simplistically stated, _____s are things of value that can be readily converted into cash.
    a. Asset
    b. A4e
    c. AAAI
    d. A Stake in the Outcome

1. _____, in microeconomics, are the cost advantages that a business obtains due to expansion. They are factors that cause a producer's average cost per unit to fall as scale is increased. _____ is a long run concept and refers to reductions in unit cost as the size of a facility, or scale, increases.
   a. A Stake in the Outcome
   b. Economies of scope
   c. A4e
   d. Economies of scale

2. Network externalities resemble economies of scale, but they are not considered such because they are a function of the number of users of a good or service in an industry, not of the production efficiency within a business. _____ are only considered examples of network externalities if they are driven by demand side economies.

   Formally, a production function is defined to have:

   - constant returns to scale if (for any constant a greater than or equal to 0)
   - increasing returns to scale if (for any constant a greater than 1)
   - decreasing returns to scale if (for any constant a greater than 1)

   where K and L are factors of production, capital and labour, respectively.

   As an example, the Cobb-Douglas functional form has constant returns to scale when the sum of the exponents adds up to one.

   a. A Stake in the Outcome
   b. AAAI
   c. A4e
   d. Economies of scale external to the firm

3. In economics, _____ are the resources employed to produce goods and services. They facilitate production but do not become part of the product (as with raw materials) or significantly transformed by the production process (as with fuel used to power machinery.) To 19th century economists, the _____ were land (natural resources, gifts from nature), labor (the ability to work), and capital goods (human-made tools and equipment.)
   a. Multifactor productivity
   b. Production function
   c. Factors of production
   d. Productive capacity

Chapter 6. Globalization

4. _____ in its literal sense is the process of transformation of local or regional phenomena into global ones. It can be described as a process by which the people of the world are unified into a single society and function together.

This process is a combination of economic, technological, sociocultural and political forces.

   a. Histogram
   b. Collaborative Planning, Forecasting and Replenishment
   c. Cost Management
   d. Globalization

5. _____ or _____ data refers to selected population characteristics as used in government, marketing or opinion research, or the _____ profiles used in such research. Note the distinction from the term 'demography' Commonly-used _____s include race, age, income, disabilities, mobility (in terms of travel time to work or number of vehicles available), educational attainment, home ownership, employment status, and even location.
   a. Adam Smith
   b. Affiliation
   c. Demographic
   d. Abraham Harold Maslow

6. _____ are conceptually similar to economies of scale. Whereas economies of scale primarily refer to efficiencies associated with supply-side changes, such as increasing or decreasing the scale of production, of a single product type, _____ refer to efficiencies primarily associated with demand-side changes, such as increasing or decreasing the scope of marketing and distribution, of different types of products. _____ are one of the main reasons for such marketing strategies as product bundling, product lining, and family branding.
   a. A4e
   b. Economies of scale
   c. A Stake in the Outcome
   d. Economies of scope

7. _____ is the term used to describe a situation where different entities cooperate advantageously for a final outcome. Simply defined, it means that the whole is greater than the sum of the individual parts. Although the whole will be greater than each individual part, this is not the concept of _____.
   a. Synergy
   b. 1990 Clean Air Act
   c. 33 Strategies of War
   d. 28-hour day

8. A _____ or transnational corporation is a corporation or enterprise that manages production or delivers services in more than one country. It can also be referred to as an international corporation.

The first modern _____ is generally thought to be the Dutch East India Company, established in 1602.

   a. Small and medium enterprises
   b. Command center
   c. Multinational corporation
   d. Financial Accounting Standards Board

9. _____ is the increase in the amount of the goods and services produced by an economy over time and is dependent on an increase in the creation of money. Growth is conventionally measured as the percent rate of increase in real gross domestic product, or real GDP. GDP is usually calculated in real terms, i.e. inflation-adjusted terms, in order to net out the effect of inflation on the price of the goods and services produced.
   a. A4e
   b. AAAI
   c. Economic growth
   d. A Stake in the Outcome

10. The _____ is the labour pool in employment. It is generally used to describe those working for a single company or industry, but can also apply to a geographic region like a city, country, state, etc. The term generally excludes the employers or management, and implies those involved in manual labour.
    a. Division of labour
    b. Pink-collar worker
    c. Work-life balance
    d. Workforce

11. The notion of _____ is found in the writings of Mikhail Bakunin, Friedrich Nietzsche, and in Werner Sombart's Krieg und Kapitalismus (War and Capitalism) (1913, p. 207), where he wrote: 'again out of destruction a new spirit of creativity arises'. In Capitalism, Socialism and Democracy, the Austrian economist Joseph Schumpeter popularized and used the term to describe the process of transformation that accompanies radical innovation.
    a. 28-hour day
    b. Creative destruction
    c. 1990 Clean Air Act
    d. 33 Strategies of War

12. In economics, _____ is the desire to own something and the ability to pay for it. The term _____ signifies the ability or the willingness to buy a particular commodity at a given point of time.

Chapter 6. Globalization

a. Demand
b. 33 Strategies of War
c. 1990 Clean Air Act
d. 28-hour day

13. _____ is exchange of capital, goods, and services across international borders or territories. In most countries, it represents a significant share of gross domestic product (GDP.) While _____ has been present throughout much of history, its economic, social, and political importance has been on the rise in recent centuries.

    a. AAAI
    b. International trade
    c. A Stake in the Outcome
    d. A4e

14. _____ is the removal or simplification of government rules and regulations that constrain the operation of market forces. _____ does not mean elimination of laws against fraud, but eliminating or reducing government control of how business is done, thereby moving toward a more free market.

The stated rationale for '_____' is often that fewer and simpler regulations will lead to a raised level of competitiveness, therefore higher productivity, more efficiency and lower prices overall.

    a. Rehn-Meidner Model
    b. Natural rate of unemployment
    c. Value added
    d. Deregulation

15. In economics, _____ refers to the ability of a person or a country to produce a particular good at a lower marginal cost and opportunity cost than another person or country. It is the ability to produce a product most efficiently given all the other products that could be produced. It can be contrasted with absolute advantage which refers to the ability of a person or a country to produce a particular good at a lower absolute cost than another.

    a. 1990 Clean Air Act
    b. Comparative advantage
    c. 33 Strategies of War
    d. 28-hour day

16. _____ is a type of trade policy that allows traders to act and transact without interference from government. Thus, the policy permits trading partners mutual gains from trade, with goods and services produced according to the theory of comparative advantage.

Under a _____ policy, prices are a reflection of true supply and demand, and are the sole determinant of resource allocation.

a. 33 Strategies of War
b. Free trade
c. 1990 Clean Air Act
d. 28-hour day

17. The _____ was the outcome of the failure of negotiating governments to create the International Trade Organization (ITO.) GATT was formed in 1947 and lasted until 1994, when it was replaced by the World Trade Organization. The Bretton Woods Conference had introduced the idea for an organization to regulate trade as part of a larger plan for economic recovery after World War II.
a. General Agreement on Tariffs and Trade
b. 1990 Clean Air Act
c. 28-hour day
d. Multilateral treaty

18. The _____ or gross domestic income (GDI), a basic measure of an economy's economic performance, is the market value of all final goods and services made within the borders of a nation in a year. _____ can be defined in three ways, all of which are conceptually identical. First, it is equal to the total expenditures for all final goods and services produced within the country in a stipulated period of time (usually a 365-day year).
a. Human capital
b. Productivity management
c. Perfect competition
d. Gross domestic product

19. In economics, business, retail, and accounting, a _____ is the value of money that has been used up to produce something, and hence is not available for use anymore. In economics, a _____ is an alternative that is given up as a result of a decision. In business, the _____ may be one of acquisition, in which case the amount of money expended to acquire it is counted as _____.
a. Cost
b. Cost allocation
c. Cost overrun
d. Fixed costs

20. The _____ is an expected return that the provider of capital plans to earn on their investment.

Capital (money) used for funding a business should earn returns for the capital providers who risk their capital. For an investment to be worthwhile, the expected return on capital must be greater than the _____.

a. Capital intensive
b. Weighted average cost of capital
c. 1990 Clean Air Act
d. Cost of capital

21. _____ is the amount of goods and services that a labourer produces in a given amount of time. It is one of several types of productivity that economists measure. _____ can be measured for a firm, a process or a country.

a. Business Network Transformation
b. Time and attendance
c. Retroactive overtime
d. Labour productivity

22. _____ refers to metrics and measures of output from production processes, per unit of input. Labor _____, for example, is typically measured as a ratio of output per labor-hour, an input. _____ may be conceived of as a metrics of the technical or engineering efficiency of production.

a. Value engineering
b. Remanufacturing
c. Master production schedule
d. Productivity

23. _____ refers to the aggregated strategies of single business firm or a strategic business unit (SBU) in a diversified corporation. According to Michael Porter, a firm must formulate a _____ that incorporates either cost leadership, differentiation or focus in order to achieve a sustainable competitive advantage and long-term success in its chosen arenas or industries.

Functional strategies include marketing strategies, new product development strategies, human resource strategies, financial strategies, legal strategies, supply-chain strategies, and information technology management strategies.

a. Competitive heterogeneity
b. Strategic thinking
c. Switching cost
d. Business strategy

Chapter 6. Globalization

24. A _____ strategy is the planned method of delivering goods or services to a target market and distributing them there. When importing or exporting services, it refers to establishing and managing contracts in a foreign country.

Many companies successfully operate in a niche market without ever expanding into new markets.

 a. Horizontal integration
 b. Foreign ownership
 c. Psychological pricing
 d. Market entry

25. _____ is an economic and social system in which trade and industry are privately controlled for profit. The means of production, which is otherwise known as capital and includes land are owned, operated, and traded for the purpose of generating profits, without force or fraud, by private individuals either singly or jointly. Investments, distribution, income, production, pricing and supply of goods, commodities and services are determined by voluntary private decision in _____, which is also known as a market economy.

 a. Affiliation
 b. Abraham Harold Maslow
 c. Adam Smith
 d. Capitalism

26. _____ of the learning curve effect and the closely related experience curve effect express the relationship between equations for experience and efficiency or between efficiency gains and investment in the effort. The experience of 'learning curves' was first observed by the 19th Century German psychologist Hermann Ebbinghaus according to the difficulty of memorizing varying numbers of verbal stimuli, and subsequent learning about the complex processes of learning are discussed in the

The rule used for representing the learning curve effect states that the more times a task has been performed, the less time will be required on each subsequent iteration.

 a. Models
 b. Point biserial correlation coefficient
 c. Spatial Decision Support Systems
 d. Distribution

27. A _____ is an entity formed between two or more parties to undertake economic activity together. The parties agree to create a new entity by both contributing equity, and they then share in the revenues, expenses, and control of the enterprise. The venture can be for one specific project only, or a continuing business relationship such as the Fuji Xerox _____.

a. Civil Rights Act of 1991
b. Joint venture
c. Patent
d. Meritor Savings Bank v. Vinson

28. _____ refers to the overarching strategy of the diversified firm. Such a _____ answers the questions of 'in which businesses should we be in?' and 'how does being in these business create synergy and/or add to the competitive advantage of the corporation as a whole?'

Business strategy refers to the aggregated strategies of single business firm or a strategic business unit (SBU) in a diversified corporation. According to Michael Porter, a firm must formulate a business strategy that incorporates either cost leadership, differentiation or focus in order to achieve a sustainable competitive advantage and long-term success in its chosen arenas or industries.

a. Corporate strategy
b. Strategic group
c. Strategic drift
d. Competitive heterogeneity

29. An _____ is a person who has possession of an enterprise and assumes significant accountability for the inherent risks and the outcome. It is an ambitious leader who combines land, labor, and capital to create and market new goods or services. The term is a loanword from French and was first defined by the Irish economist Richard Cantillon.

a. AAAI
b. Entrepreneur
c. A Stake in the Outcome
d. A4e

30. _____ in manufacturing refers to processes that occur later on in a production sequence or production line.

Viewing a company 'from order to cash' might have high-level processes such as Marketing, Sales, Order Entry, Manufacturing, Packaging, Shipping, Invoicing. Each of these could be deconstructed into many sub-processes and supporting processes.

a. Genbutsu
b. Downstream
c. Science Learning Centre
d. Probability-generating function

Chapter 6. Globalization

31. In microeconomics and management, the term _____ describes a style of management control. Vertically integrated companies are united through a hierarchy with a common owner. Usually each member of the hierarchy produces a different product or (market-specific) service, and the products combine to satisfy a common need.
   a. Vertical integration
   b. 28-hour day
   c. 1990 Clean Air Act
   d. 33 Strategies of War

32. _____ as defined in business terms is an organization's strategic guide to globalization. A sound _____ should address these questions: what must be (versus what is) the extent of market presence in the world's major markets? How to build the necessary global presence? What must be (versus what is) the optimal locations around the world for the various value chain activities? How to run global presence into global competitive advantage?

   Academic research on _____ came of age during the 1980s, including work by Michael Porter and Christopher Bartlett ' Sumantra Ghoshal. Among the forces perceived to bring about the globalization of competition were convergence in economic systems and technological change, especially in information technology, that facilitated and required the coordination of a multinational firm's strategy on a worldwide scale.

   a. 28-hour day
   b. 33 Strategies of War
   c. 1990 Clean Air Act
   d. Global strategy

33. _____ consists of the mental process of thinking involved with the process of judging the merits of multiple options and selecting one of them for action. Some simple examples include deciding whether to get up in the morning or go back to sleep, or selecting a given route for a journey. More complex examples (often decisions that affect what a person thinks or their core beliefs) include choosing a lifestyle, religious affiliation, or political position.
   a. Championship mobilization
   b. Trade study
   c. Choice
   d. Groups decision making

34. _____ refers to the methods of practicing and using another person's business philosophy. The franchisor grants the independent operator the right to distribute its products, techniques, and trademarks for a percentage of gross monthly sales and a royalty fee. Various tangibles and intangibles such as national or international advertising, training, and other support services are commonly made available by the franchisor.

a. 28-hour day
b. 1990 Clean Air Act
c. ServiceMaster
d. Franchising

35. _____ is subcontracting a process, such as product design or manufacturing, to a third-party company. The decision to outsource is often made in the interest of lowering cost or making better use of time and energy costs, redirecting or conserving energy directed at the competencies of a particular business, or to make more efficient use of land, labor, capital, (information) technology and resources. _____ became part of the business lexicon during the 1980s.

   a. Unemployment insurance
   b. Opinion leadership
   c. Outsourcing
   d. Operant conditioning

36. The _____ is a concept from business management that was first described and popularized by Michael Porter in his 1985 best-seller, Competitive Advantage: Creating and Sustaining Superior Performance.

A _____ is a chain of activities. Products pass through all activities of the chain in order and at each activity the product gains some value. The chain of activities gives the products more added value than the sum of added values of all activities. It is important not to mix the concept of the _____ with the costs occurring throughout the activities.

   a. Market development
   b. Mass marketing
   c. Customer relationship management
   d. Value chain

Chapter 7. Innovation and Entrepreneurship

1. _____ according to Onuoha (2007) is the practice of starting new organizations or revitalizing mature organizations, particularly new businesses generally in response to identified opportunities. _____ is often a difficult undertaking, as a vast majority of new businesses fail. Entrepreneurial activities are substantially different depending on the type of organization that is being started.
   a. AAAI
   b. A4e
   c. A Stake in the Outcome
   d. Entrepreneurship

2. The notion of _____ is found in the writings of Mikhail Bakunin, Friedrich Nietzsche, and in Werner Sombart's Krieg und Kapitalismus (War and Capitalism) (1913, p. 207), where he wrote: 'again out of destruction a new spirit of creativity arises'. In Capitalism, Socialism and Democracy, the Austrian economist Joseph Schumpeter popularized and used the term to describe the process of transformation that accompanies radical innovation.
   a. 1990 Clean Air Act
   b. 28-hour day
   c. 33 Strategies of War
   d. Creative destruction

3. An _____ is a person who has possession of an enterprise and assumes significant accountability for the inherent risks and the outcome. It is an ambitious leader who combines land, labor, and capital to create and market new goods or services. The term is a loanword from French and was first defined by the Irish economist Richard Cantillon.
   a. A4e
   b. AAAI
   c. A Stake in the Outcome
   d. Entrepreneur

4. _____ is a type of private equity capital typically provided to early-stage, high-potential, growth companies in the interest of generating a return through an eventual realization event such as an IPO or trade sale of the company. _____ investments are generally made as cash in exchange for shares in the invested company. It is typical for _____ investors to identify and back companies in high technology industries such as biotechnology and ICT.
   a. Seed round
   b. Limited liability corporation
   c. Private equity
   d. Venture capital

5. Organizational culture is not the same as _____. It is wider and deeper concepts, something that an organization 'is' rather than what it 'has' (according to Buchanan and Huczynski.)

_____ is the total sum of the values, customs, traditions and meanings that make a company unique.

Chapter 7. Innovation and Entrepreneurship

a. Job analysis
b. Path-goal theory
c. Corporate culture
d. Work design

6. A _____ is a process in which a potential employee is evaluated by an employer for prospective employment in their company, organization and was established in the late 16th century.

A _____ typically precedes the hiring decision, and is used to evaluate the candidate. The interview is usually preceded by the evaluation of submitted résumés from interested candidates, then selecting a small number of candidates for interviews.

a. Supported employment
b. Job interview
c. Split shift
d. Payrolling

7. A _____ is a formal statement of a set of business goals, the reasons why they are believed attainable, and the plan for reaching those goals. It may also contain background information about the organization or team attempting to reach those goals.

The business goals may be defined for for-profit or for non-profit organizations.

a. Distributed management
b. Crisis management
c. Time management
d. Business plan

8. _____ , also referred to simply as a 'public offering' or 'flotation,' is when a company issues common stock or shares to the public for the first time. They are often issued by smaller, younger companies seeking capital to expand, but can also be done by large privately-owned companies looking to become publicly traded.

In an _____ the issuer may obtain the assistance of an underwriting firm, which helps it determine what type of security to issue (common or preferred), best offering price and time to bring it to market.

Chapter 7. Innovation and Entrepreneurship

  a. Unemployment insurance
  b. Initial public offering
  c. Outsourcing
  d. Occupational Safety and Health Administration

9. An _____ is any party that makes an investment.

The term has taken on a specific meaning in finance to describe the particular types of people and companies that regularly purchase equity or debt securities for financial gain in exchange for funding an expanding company. Less frequently, the term is applied to parties who purchase real estate, currency, commodity derivatives, personal property, or other assets.

  a. AAAI
  b. A4e
  c. A Stake in the Outcome
  d. Investor

10. _____ is the increase in the amount of the goods and services produced by an economy over time and is dependent on an increase in the creation of money. Growth is conventionally measured as the percent rate of increase in real gross domestic product, or real GDP. GDP is usually calculated in real terms, i.e. inflation-adjusted terms, in order to net out the effect of inflation on the price of the goods and services produced.

  a. AAAI
  b. Economic growth
  c. A Stake in the Outcome
  d. A4e

11. _____ is the process of estimation in unknown situations. Prediction is a similar, but more general term. Both can refer to estimation of time series, cross-sectional or longitudinal data.

  a. 33 Strategies of War
  b. Forecasting
  c. 1990 Clean Air Act
  d. 28-hour day

12. _____ was a Scottish moral philosopher and a pioneer of political economy. One of the key figures of the Scottish Enlightenment, Smith is the author of The Theory of Moral Sentiments and An Inquiry into the Nature and Causes of the Wealth of Nations. The latter, usually abbreviated as The Wealth of Nations, is considered his magnum opus and the first modern work of economics.

a. Affirmative action
b. Affiliation
c. Adam Smith
d. Abraham Harold Maslow

13. The term '_____' refers to the concept of collecting information and attempting to spot a pattern in the information. In some fields of study, the term '_____' has more formally-defined meanings.

In project management _____ is a mathematical technique that uses historical results to predict future outcome.

a. Regression analysis
b. Least squares
c. Stepwise regression
d. Trend analysis

14. _____ is the removal or simplification of government rules and regulations that constrain the operation of market forces. _____ does not mean elimination of laws against fraud, but eliminating or reducing government control of how business is done, thereby moving toward a more free market.

The stated rationale for '_____' is often that fewer and simpler regulations will lead to a raised level of competitiveness, therefore higher productivity, more efficiency and lower prices overall.

a. Natural rate of unemployment
b. Deregulation
c. Value added
d. Rehn-Meidner Model

15. The _____ is a systematic, interactive forecasting method which relies on a panel of independent experts. The carefully selected experts answer questionnaires in two or more rounds. After each round, a facilitator provides an anonymous summary of the experts' forecasts from the previous round as well as the reasons they provided for their judgments.

a. Learning organization
b. Quality function deployment
c. Hoshin Kanri
d. Delphi method

Chapter 7. Innovation and Entrepreneurship

16. The _____ was a period in the late 18th and early 19th centuries when major changes in agriculture, manufacturing, mining, and transportation had a profound effect on the socioeconomic and cultural conditions in Britain. The changes subsequently spread throughout Europe, North America, and eventually the world. The onset of the _____ marked a major turning point in human society; almost every aspect of daily life was eventually influenced in some way.

   a. Abraham Harold Maslow
   b. Adam Smith
   c. Affiliation
   d. Industrial Revolution

17. _____ is technology based on biology, especially when used in agriculture, food science, and medicine. United Nations Convention on Biological Diversity defines _____ as:

_____ is often used to refer to genetic engineering technology of the 21st century, however the term encompasses a wider range and history of procedures for modifying biological organisms according to the needs of humanity, going back to the initial modifications of native plants into improved food crops through artificial selection and hybridization. Bioengineering is the science upon which all biotechnological applications are based.

   a. Biotechnology
   b. 33 Strategies of War
   c. 1990 Clean Air Act
   d. 28-hour day

18. _____ of the learning curve effect and the closely related experience curve effect express the relationship between equations for experience and efficiency or between efficiency gains and investment in the effort. The experience of 'learning curves' was first observed by the 19th Century German psychologist Hermann Ebbinghaus according to the difficulty of memorizing varying numbers of verbal stimuli, and subsequent learning about the complex processes of learning are discussed in the

The rule used for representing the learning curve effect states that the more times a task has been performed, the less time will be required on each subsequent iteration.

   a. Point biserial correlation coefficient
   b. Models
   c. Distribution
   d. Spatial Decision Support Systems

19. In decision theory and estimation theory, the _____ of an estimator, $\hat{\theta}$, of an unknown parameter of the distribution, θ, is the expected value of the loss function

$$R(\theta, \hat{\theta}) = \mathbb{E}_\theta L(\theta, \hat{\theta}) = \int L(\theta, \hat{\theta})\, dP_\theta.$$

where dP_θ is a probability measure parametrized by θ.

- For a scalar parameter θ and a quadratic loss function,

$$L(\theta, \hat{\theta}) = (\theta - \hat{\theta})^2$$

the _____ function becomes the mean squared error of the estimate,

$$R(\theta, \hat{\theta}) = E_\theta(\theta - \hat{\theta})^2$$

- In density estimation, the unknown parameter is probability density itself. The loss function is typically chosen to be a norm in an appropriate function space. For example, for L^2 norm,

$$L(f, \hat{f}) = \|f - \hat{f}\|_2^2$$

the _____ function becomes the mean integrated squared error

$$R(f, \hat{f}) = E\|f - \hat{f}\|^2$$

a. Financial modeling
b. Risk aversion
c. Linear model
d. Risk

20. _____ is the intelligence of machines and the branch of computer science which aims to create it. Major _____ textbooks define the field as 'the study and design of intelligent agents,' where an intelligent agent is a system that perceives its environment and takes actions which maximize its chances of success. John McCarthy, who coined the term in 1956, defines it as 'the science and engineering of making intelligent machines.'

The field was founded on the claim that a central property of human beings, intelligence--the sapience of Homo sapiens--can be so precisely described that it can be simulated by a machine.

a. A4e
b. A Stake in the Outcome
c. AAAI
d. Artificial intelligence

21. An _____ is software that attempts to reproduce the performance of one or more human experts, most commonly in a specific problem domain, and is a traditional application and/or subfield of artificial intelligence. A wide variety of methods can be used to simulate the performance of the expert however common to most or all are 1) the creation of a so-called 'knowledgebase' which uses some knowledge representation formalism to capture the Subject Matter Experts (SME) knowledge and 2) a process of gathering that knowledge from the SME and codifying it according to the formalism, which is called knowledge engineering. _____s may or may not have learning components but a third common element is that once the system is developed it is proven by being placed in the same real world problem solving situation as the human SME, typically as an aid to human workers or a supplement to some information system.
    a. A Stake in the Outcome
    b. A4e
    c. Expert System
    d. AAAI

22. The _____ is given by the United States National Institute of Standards and Technology. Through the actions of the National Productivity Advisory Committee chaired by Jack Grayson, it was established by the Malcolm Baldrige National Quality Improvement Act of 1987 - Public Law 100-107 and named for Malcolm Baldrige, who served as United States Secretary of Commerce during the Reagan administration from 1981 until his 1987 death in a rodeo accident. APQC, , organized the first White House Conference on Productivity, spearheading the creation and design of the _____ in 1987, and jointly administering the award for its first three years.
    a. Time and attendance
    b. Malcolm Baldrige National Quality Award
    c. Business Network Transformation
    d. Scenario planning

23. _____ is the process by which a new idea or new product is accepted by the market. The rate of _____ is the speed that the new idea spreads from one consumer to the next. Adoption is similar to _____ except that it deals with the psychological processes an individual goes through, rather than an aggregate market process.
    a. Category management
    b. Value chain
    c. Mass marketing
    d. Diffusion

Chapter 8. Continuous Reinvention

1. In probability theory, a probability distribution is called _____ if its cumulative distribution function is _____. This is equivalent to saying that for random variables X with the distribution in question, Pr[X = a] = 0 for all real numbers a, i.e.: the probability that X attains the value a is zero, for any number a. If the distribution of X is _____ then X is called a _____ random variable.
    a. Pay Band
    b. Connectionist expert systems
    c. Continuous
    d. Decision tree pruning

2. _____ is, in very basic words, a position a firm occupies against its competitors.

According to Michael Porter, the three methods for creating a sustainable _____ are through:

1. Cost leadership

2. Differentiation

3. Focus (economics)

    a. 1990 Clean Air Act
    b. Competitive advantage
    c. 28-hour day
    d. Theory Z

3. _____ refers to the aggregated strategies of single business firm or a strategic business unit (SBU) in a diversified corporation. According to Michael Porter, a firm must formulate a _____ that incorporates either cost leadership, differentiation or focus in order to achieve a sustainable competitive advantage and long-term success in its chosen arenas or industries.

Functional strategies include marketing strategies, new product development strategies, human resource strategies, financial strategies, legal strategies, supply-chain strategies, and information technology management strategies.

    a. Business strategy
    b. Switching cost
    c. Competitive heterogeneity
    d. Strategic thinking

4. The _____ requires the Federal government to investigate and pursue trusts, companies and organizations suspected of violating the Act. It was the first United States Federal statute to limit cartels and monopolies, and today still forms the basis for most antitrust litigation by the federal government.

Chapter 8. Continuous Reinvention

a. 28-hour day
b. 1990 Clean Air Act
c. 33 Strategies of War
d. Sherman Antitrust Act

5. _____ is a structured approach to transitioning individuals, teams, and organizations from a current state to a desired future state. The current definition of _____ includes both organizational _____ processes and individual _____ models, which together are used to manage the people side of change.

A number of models are available for understanding the transitioning of individuals through the phases of _____ and strengthening organizational development initiative in both government and corporate sectors.

a. 1990 Clean Air Act
b. 28-hour day
c. Change management
d. 33 Strategies of War

6. In decision theory and estimation theory, the _____ of an estimator, $\hat{\theta}$, of an unknown parameter of the distribution, θ, is the expected value of the loss function

$$R(\theta, \hat{\theta}) = \mathbb{E}_\theta L(\theta, \hat{\theta}) = \int L(\theta, \hat{\theta})\, dP_\theta.$$

where dP_θ is a probability measure parametrized by θ.

- For a scalar parameter θ and a quadratic loss function,

$$L(\theta, \hat{\theta}) = (\theta - \hat{\theta})^2$$

the _____ function becomes the mean squared error of the estimate,

$$R(\theta, \hat{\theta}) = E_\theta (\theta - \hat{\theta})^2$$

- In density estimation, the unknown parameter is probability density itself. The loss function is typically chosen to be a norm in an appropriate function space. For example, for L^2 norm,

$$L(f, \hat{f}) = \|f - \hat{f}\|_2^2$$

the _____ function becomes the mean integrated squared error

$$R(f, \hat{f}) = E\|f - \hat{f}\|^2$$

a. Financial modeling
b. Linear model
c. Risk aversion
d. Risk

7. _____ is a term used in project management and business administration to describe a process where all the individuals or groups that are likely to be affected by the activities of a project are identified and then sorted according to how much they can affect the project and how much the project can affect them. This information is used to assess how the interests of those stakeholders should be addressed in the project plan.

A stakeholder is any person or organization, who can be positively or negatively impacted by, or cause an impact on the actions of a company.

a. Stakeholder analysis
b. 33 Strategies of War
c. 1990 Clean Air Act
d. 28-hour day

Chapter 8. Continuous Reinvention

8. The _____ is a concept from business management that was first described and popularized by Michael Porter in his 1985 best-seller, Competitive Advantage: Creating and Sustaining Superior Performance.

A _____ is a chain of activities. Products pass through all activities of the chain in order and at each activity the product gains some value. The chain of activities gives the products more added value than the sum of added values of all activities. It is important not to mix the concept of the _____ with the costs occurring throughout the activities.

  a. Mass marketing
  b. Market development
  c. Customer relationship management
  d. Value chain

9. _____ consists of the mental process of thinking involved with the process of judging the merits of multiple options and selecting one of them for action. Some simple examples include deciding whether to get up in the morning or go back to sleep, or selecting a given route for a journey. More complex examples (often decisions that affect what a person thinks or their core beliefs) include choosing a lifestyle, religious affiliation, or political position.
  a. Championship mobilization
  b. Trade study
  c. Choice
  d. Groups decision making

10. The _____ of a statistical model describes how well it fits a set of observations. Measures of _____ typically summarize the discrepancy between observed values and the values expected under the model in question. Such measures can be used in statistical hypothesis testing, e.g. to test for normality of residuals, to test whether two samples are drawn from identical distributions , or whether outcome frequencies follow a specified distribution
  a. Law of the iterated logarithm
  b. Location-scale family
  c. Pareto Analysis
  d. Goodness of fit

11. The _____ is an economic tool used to determine the strategic resources available to a firm. The fundamental principle of the _____ is that the basis for a competitive advantage of a firm lies primarily in the application of the bundle of valuable resources at the firm's disposal (Wernerfelt, 1984, p172; Rumelt, 1984, p557-558.) To transform a short-run competitive advantage into a sustained competitive advantage requires that these resources are heterogeneous in nature and not perfectly mobile (Barney, 1991, p105-106; Peteraf, 1993, p180).

a. Catfish effect
b. Frenemy
c. Business philosophy
d. Resource-based view

12. The phrase mergers and _____s refers to the aspect of corporate strategy, corporate finance and management dealing with the buying, selling and combining of different companies that can aid, finance, or help a growing company in a given industry grow rapidly without having to create another business entity.

An _____, also known as a takeover or a buyout, is the buying of one company (the 'target') by another. An _____ may be friendly or hostile.

   a. A Stake in the Outcome
   b. Acquisition
   c. AAAI
   d. A4e

13. In finance and economics, _____ or divestiture is the reduction of some kind of asset for either financial or ethical objectives or sale of an existing business by a firm. A _____ is the opposite of an investment.
   a. 28-hour day
   b. 1990 Clean Air Act
   c. Divestment
   d. 33 Strategies of War

14. _____ according to Onuoha (2007) is the practice of starting new organizations or revitalizing mature organizations, particularly new businesses generally in response to identified opportunities. _____ is often a difficult undertaking, as a vast majority of new businesses fail. Entrepreneurial activities are substantially different depending on the type of organization that is being started.
   a. A Stake in the Outcome
   b. AAAI
   c. A4e
   d. Entrepreneurship

15. _____ as defined in business terms is an organization's strategic guide to globalization. A sound _____ should address these questions: what must be (versus what is) the extent of market presence in the world's major markets? How to build the necessary global presence? What must be (versus what is) the optimal locations around the world for the various value chain activities? How to run global presence into global competitive advantage?

Academic research on _____ came of age during the 1980s, including work by Michael Porter and Christopher Bartlett ' Sumantra Ghoshal. Among the forces perceived to bring about the globalization of competition were convergence in economic systems and technological change, especially in information technology, that facilitated and required the coordination of a multinational firm's strategy on a worldwide scale.

- a. 33 Strategies of War
- b. 1990 Clean Air Act
- c. 28-hour day
- d. Global strategy

16. _____ is subcontracting a process, such as product design or manufacturing, to a third-party company. The decision to outsource is often made in the interest of lowering cost or making better use of time and energy costs, redirecting or conserving energy directed at the competencies of a particular business, or to make more efficient use of land, labor, capital, (information) technology and resources. _____ became part of the business lexicon during the 1980s.
- a. Operant conditioning
- b. Outsourcing
- c. Opinion leadership
- d. Unemployment insurance

17. In marketing, _____ has come to mean the process by which marketers try to create an image or identity in the minds of their target market for its product, brand, or organization. It is the 'relative competitive comparison' their product occupies in a given market as perceived by the target market.

Re-_____ involves changing the identity of a product, relative to the identity of competing products, in the collective minds of the target market.

- a. Positioning
- b. Context analysis
- c. PEST analysis
- d. Customer analytics

18. The notion of _____ is found in the writings of Mikhail Bakunin, Friedrich Nietzsche, and in Werner Sombart's Krieg und Kapitalismus (War and Capitalism) (1913, p. 207), where he wrote: 'again out of destruction a new spirit of creativity arises'. In Capitalism, Socialism and Democracy, the Austrian economist Joseph Schumpeter popularized and used the term to describe the process of transformation that accompanies radical innovation.

Chapter 8. Continuous Reinvention

a. Creative destruction
b. 28-hour day
c. 1990 Clean Air Act
d. 33 Strategies of War

19. _____ or _____ data refers to selected population characteristics as used in government, marketing or opinion research, or the _____ profiles used in such research. Note the distinction from the term 'demography' Commonly-used _____ s include race, age, income, disabilities, mobility (in terms of travel time to work or number of vehicles available), educational attainment, home ownership, employment status, and even location.

a. Abraham Harold Maslow
b. Affiliation
c. Demographic
d. Adam Smith

20. _____ is a joint trade and industry body working towards making the grocery sector as a whole more responsive to consumer demand and promote the removal of unnecessary costs from the supply chain.

The _____ movement beginning in the mid-nineties was characterized by the emergence of new principles of collaborative management along the supply chain. It was understood that companies can serve consumers better, faster and at less cost by working together with trading partners.

a. Efficient consumer response
b. Exception management
c. Event management
d. Entertainment Management

21. _____ describes the situation when output from (or information about the result of) an event or phenomenon in the past will influence the same event/phenomenon in the present or future. When an event is part of a chain of cause-and-effect that forms a circuit or loop, then the event is said to 'feed back' into itself.

_____ is also a synonym for:

- _____ signal; the information about the initial event that is the basis for subsequent modification of the event.
- _____ loop; the causal path that leads from the initial generation of the _____ signal to the subsequent modification of the event.

_____ is a mechanism, process or signal that is looped back to control a system within itself. Such a loop is called a _____ loop.

a. 1990 Clean Air Act
b. Feedback
c. Feedback loop
d. Positive feedback

22. Feedback describes the situation when output from (or information about the result of) an event or phenomenon in the past will influence the same event/phenomenon in the present or future. When an event is part of a chain of cause-and-effect that forms a circuit or loop, then the event is said to 'feed back' into itself.

Feedback is also a synonym for:

- Feedback signal; the information about the initial event that is the basis for subsequent modification of the event.
- _____; the causal path that leads from the initial generation of the feedback signal to the subsequent modification of the event.

Feedback is a mechanism, process or signal that is looped back to control a system within itself. Such a loop is called a _____.

a. Negative feedback
b. Positive feedback
c. 1990 Clean Air Act
d. Feedback loop

23. _____ is a broad label that refers to any individuals or households that use goods and services generated within the economy. The concept of a _____ is used in different contexts, so that the usage and significance of the term may vary.

Typically when business people and economists talk of _____s they are talking about person as _____, an aggregated commodity item with little individuality other than that expressed in the buy/not-buy decision.

a. 33 Strategies of War
b. 28-hour day
c. 1990 Clean Air Act
d. Consumer

24. _____ is one of the four elements of marketing mix. An organization or set of organizations (go-betweens) involved in the process of making a product or service available for use or consumption by a consumer or business user.

The other three parts of the marketing mix are product, pricing, and promotion.

a. Missing completely at random
b. Matching theory
c. Job creation programs
d. Distribution

ANSWER KEY

Chapter 1
1. d	2. b	3. d	4. a	5. a	6. d	7. a	8. d	9. d	10. b
11. c	12. b	13. a	14. d	15. d	16. d	17. d	18. a	19. d	20. d
21. b	22. d	23. a	24. d	25. d	26. d	27. b	28. a	29. b	30. a
31. d									

Chapter 2
1. a	2. b	3. d	4. b	5. b	6. c	7. d	8. c	9. a	10. d
11. d	12. c	13. d	14. d	15. a	16. b	17. d	18. b	19. b	20. a
21. a	22. a	23. d	24. d	25. b	26. d	27. d	28. b	29. d	30. c
31. b	32. d	33. d	34. d	35. a	36. a	37. b	38. a	39. a	40. d
41. a	42. d	43. d							

Chapter 3
1. d	2. d	3. b	4. c	5. d	6. b	7. d	8. a	9. a	10. d
11. b	12. d	13. c	14. a	15. b	16. d	17. d	18. d	19. d	20. d
21. b	22. d	23. d	24. d	25. a	26. c	27. c	28. b	29. d	30. d
31. d	32. d	33. c							

Chapter 4
1. d	2. d	3. d	4. b	5. a	6. d	7. a	8. d	9. c	10. c
11. d	12. c	13. d	14. d	15. b	16. d	17. d	18. a	19. d	20. d
21. b	22. d	23. c							

Chapter 5
1. d	2. b	3. b	4. d	5. c	6. d	7. d	8. d	9. d	10. a
11. d	12. d	13. d	14. b	15. b	16. d	17. b	18. d	19. a	20. b
21. d	22. b	23. a	24. b	25. d	26. d	27. a	28. b	29. d	30. b
31. c	32. a								

Chapter 6
1. d	2. d	3. c	4. d	5. c	6. d	7. a	8. c	9. c	10. d
11. b	12. a	13. b	14. d	15. b	16. b	17. a	18. d	19. a	20. d
21. d	22. d	23. d	24. d	25. d	26. a	27. b	28. a	29. b	30. b
31. a	32. d	33. c	34. d	35. c	36. d				

Chapter 7
1. d	2. d	3. d	4. d	5. c	6. b	7. d	8. b	9. d	10. b
11. b	12. c	13. d	14. b	15. d	16. d	17. a	18. b	19. d	20. d
21. c	22. b	23. d							

Chapter 8
1. c	2. b	3. a	4. d	5. c	6. d	7. a	8. d	9. c	10. d
11. d	12. b	13. c	14. d	15. d	16. b	17. a	18. a	19. c	20. a
21. b	22. d	23. d	24. d						